CALL
ME
NIKKI

Nikki Navarro

CALL ME NIKKI

*One Woman's Battle to Find Freedom
and Break the Cycle of Abuse*

GOLDEN FORTUNE
PRODUCTIONS

Published by Golden Fortune Productions, Dallas County, Texas
https://traumabooknikki.com/

Edited and designed by Girl Friday Productions
www.girlfridayproductions.com

Cover design: David Fassett
Project management: Reshma Kooner
Editorial production: Abi Pollokoff

ISBN (paperback): 979-8-9874973-0-2
ISBN (ebook): 979-8-9874973-1-9

To my dear princess Little Nikki—I dedicate this book to you, for you are very much a part of me. I promise to hold your hand every time you fear, and I'll be there before the next teardrop falls.

To my sons—I love you dearly.

To Renee, my therapist—a good therapist is hard to find and hard to part ways with. Thank you.

To Melissa—thanks for representing me. You propelled me to change, even though it took me time to see the fruits growing from the seeds of encouragement. Forever grateful.

To the travelers and strangers on my life's journey who provided me a glimpse of a bright ray of love through the eyes of compassion—it is through you kind souls that my broken, shattered Nikki was able to witness true, unconditional love.

To all the victims and survivors of abuse and trauma—this is to inspire you to reach within, find strength to reinvent yourself, conquer adversity with a deep passion, and make lasting changes to break generations of dysfunction and find healing from the power of love that's inside each of you.

CONTENTS

PROLOGUE

Have you ever been determined to do something, anything that was absolutely worthwhile, and told yourself confidently, *I am going to do this*, but when push came to shove, you didn't? Perhaps, time and again, words do not meet actions for you, despite your best intentions. This is how it was with me for much of my life. See, my mind absolutely believed I could achieve a goal or make a big change, but my heart was so wounded that I couldn't. My mind wanted to accomplish so much, but my heart did not believe I was capable. This kept me grounded for many years, my wings viciously clipped by the violence I endured and my own doubt about my abilities.

I was physically and emotionally abused since I was a small child, and shame, pain, and guilt were deeply rooted in my mind. I thought I did not deserve a good, loving partner, and I made poor choices in relationships. Up until a few years ago, I thought I was a failure. I was stuck in a negative belief system that had been ingrained in my mind in childhood. I have traveled a long journey of pain and bad choices since then. I held on to all of it, deep down in my soul, and these feelings took root and turned into anger and bitterness. They prevented me from moving forward, allowing my husbands to control me as my mother and my childhood abusers once had. I thought this was what I deserved, subconsciously at least, but today I know better. I know myself, I know what I've accomplished, and I know that I deserve love. I will never go back to doubting myself.

With the help of my therapist, I faced my trauma head-on and handed over all that pain, shame, and guilt to my abusers—where it always belonged. I've traveled this journey of mine for more than fifty years, and those awful memories are now a part of myself that I embrace. They are part of my power. I used them as a catalyst to create a new me, someone who stands up for herself and makes sure her voice is heard. The new me has grown back her wings, and I soar freely above everything that once held me down. No one controls me now except me. And all that pain? Those wounds I carried deep within my soul for so many years? I now see them as a part of my story, and it's one with a happy ending.

I've gone from victim to survivor to warrior and am currently thriving as an entrepreneur. This is my story, and every wound, every happy moment, every abuse, every kind interaction, every time I thought I wasn't enough, every triumph, every failure—it is all me.

I hope sharing what I've gone through inspires people in situations that feel out of their control. People who feel stuck in the loop of bad decisions they've made. People dealing with feelings of rage and inadequacy, whether it be from childhood traumas or other experiences. I believe that we are all links in a chain of wounded souls, that we all carry shame, guilt, and anger from violence that's been enacted upon us. Those feelings get repressed, pushing us to make unhealthy decisions for ourselves and the people around us, keeping us all trapped in a cycle of generational violence and harm.

Silence empowers that vicious cycle, so this book is my way of breaking the silence, breaking the chains that have held down me, my family, and so many others across generations. My main message for you, dear reader, is this: though we all need some help to get there, empowerment comes from within. Whoever you dream of being, that person is already inside you. Whatever you dream of achieving, I promise you, it is possible. You are enough.

If I can do it, so can you. Let's fly together.

PART ONE

1968 to 1988

1

Passing Down Trauma

Violence is woven throughout most of my childhood memories. Chaos and abuse were the norm in my dysfunctional family. It was part of a cycle that spanned generations, repeated endlessly from one to the next. Some might call it a curse. All I knew was that my mother, Julie, was a very angry woman, and she often took her rage out on me. I've suppressed much of what happened to me when I was young and defenseless, but every so often, another traumatic memory breaks through my protective mental shield. Maybe my subconscious thinks I'm strong enough to handle the memories now. They still hurt, though, even after all these years.

Julie's wrath was a frightening thing to behold, and I still bear the scars from one particularly brutal encounter, a daily reminder of how much my mother hated me. It was a chilly spring day, and I was about three years old. My mother was making *caldo de pollo*, a hearty Mexican soup, furiously throwing carrots, potatoes, and cabbage into a simmering pot on the stove, when I asked her if I could go play outside. I'd do anything to get away from the torment I was living inside those walls. It was the weekend, and my stepfather Jack had just given Mom another one of his beatings.

I often found myself staring out our living room window and watching other, happy families with dogs and smiling moms and dads live lives I wished I were living. I would see the little redheaded girl with freckles who lived across the street leave her house with her mom and wish I was her. I dreamed of having a loving family. This little girl, whose name I can't recall, was so sweet. She saw me crying once and brought me cake and cookies, which is how we became friends. But my mother didn't let me go outside to play very often. Perhaps she thought all those dark secrets in our home would spill out of me if I were shown the slightest bit of kindness or compassion. Mom had no friends of her own. She had trouble getting along with others, perhaps because her own abusive childhood left her too emotionally stunted to let anyone in. In retrospect, I realize that maybe I should have known not to approach her; she was clearly in a terrible mood. She hated cooking, hated being a caretaker—having been one since she was a child herself. But then again, I don't recall my mother ever being in a *good* mood. And how was I to know all this when I was just a child myself?

"Out of my way, stupid girl," she yelled at me. I started crying and tried to hug her, but she pushed me away. She took the ladle she'd been using to stir the big silver pot of soup, which was now boiling and gurgling, and smacked me on the head with it. The boiling water scalded my scalp so deeply that to this day, there is a quarter-size bald spot where my hair just won't grow. What's even worse is she told my grandmother that it was *my* fault, that I was a needy, fussy girl, and I got too close to her when she was cooking the soup, and the boiling water bubbled over, burning my scalp. Every time I do my hair, I am reminded that I survived my childhood.

Julie, Jack, my younger half brother, and I lived in a small one-bedroom wood-frame house in Fremont, Ohio, at the time. I slept on a mattress in a little studio, a room that never seemed to get warm enough during the winter months. The house was an old cottage with lots of cracks where the cold air would seep in; some of the windowpanes were broken, the wood floors were bare, and our aging heaters just couldn't seem to chase the chill away. It was an old and dilapidated home as cold as the unloving atmosphere. I spent a lot of time there wishing everything I was experiencing was just a bad dream. I lived in my own little world, trying to shield myself from all the abuse and anger I saw inside those walls.

I used to dream about meeting my biological father, wondering why he wasn't in my life. Whenever I asked my mother about him, she chastised me, called me stupid, an idiot. I have often wondered whether I look like him—I don't know because I've never met him or seen a photo—and perhaps my face reminded her of him. She told me that my father never cared for me or loved me, that I was unwanted, that she hated me and didn't want me in her face. She never even told me his name until I was in the fourth grade, but by then I had figured it out for myself. I'd go into her old purses and dig up information when she wasn't around, and one time I found my birth certificate with his first name on it, though it was the Spanish version: Pedro.

Her anger at my biological father had hardened into hate, and I was the target. She was spiteful toward me from a young age, rarely acknowledging my successes or even my presence, much less giving me the love I craved. I learned to tiptoe around her, constantly trying to please her and never knowing why I couldn't. My mother always seemed to have a reason to find fault in me. I felt like there must be something wrong with me if the two people who'd created me didn't love me or even want me. Like so many children who experience abuse, I blamed myself. It didn't help that I was constantly witnessing—and then experiencing—violence because Jack, who was only the first of my stepfathers, had a terrible temper.

My mother worked long hours at a doughnut shop in town, even on the weekends. Jack worked nights for the Cincinnati, Sandusky and Cleveland Railroad Company and would watch me on the days my mom worked. My memories of him are faint and spotty, but this is the detail about him that stands out most clearly: he was a monster in more ways than one, and the first of many who would come into my life.

One wintry Sunday afternoon, I wistfully watched my mom through the window as she made her way to our home. More than anything at this age, I longed for my mom to be close to me, to feel that she loved me. I heard her go into the kitchen and ask Jack why he hadn't made dinner. The next thing I heard was my mother's screams. I opened the old screechy wood door of my room and saw Jack with his hand on the buckle of his leather belt, pulling it out of the loops of his pants. My mom fought back against him, but he was bigger than her, stronger. He overpowered her, wrestling her to the floor with the belt in his hand. I can still see her, vividly, crying on the kitchen floor, but the detail I remember most is how their eyes looked as they stared at each other, how both their faces were overtaken by an evil rage so forceful they almost seemed demonic. I was helpless to do anything, terrified of what would happen next.

It was in these moments of shattered calm in a broken home that Little Nikki was born. Little Nikki is the name I've given to my inner child. My sweet princess Little Nikki was innocent from the start, deserving of protection and desperate for love. When I experienced any kind of pain or terror, Little Nikki would be there to take over those feelings, protecting me as much as she could. Certainly, though, she was the child who watched Jack abuse my mother, who would herself become a victim of that abuse before my mother found the strength to cut him out of our lives.

***

Like so many of the women in my family, my mother did not have an easy life when she was growing up. Julie was the third-eldest daughter of my grandmother's nine children, one of whom—one twin baby girl—died soon after her birth. Four of her siblings had different fathers. My mom was the product of a short-lived affair between my grandmother and Roberto Robles. They'd met at El Robles, one of the bars he owned, and not long afterward, my grandmother found out she was pregnant. Roberto tried to be a part of my mother's life, but he was married to another woman at the time, so maybe that's why my grandmother spurned his attempts to connect with my mother. However, Roberto did step up and offer monetary support.

It's no wonder my grandmother was cold and bitter. My grandmother never had the chance to get an education, and though she was a fierce woman with a strong warrior spirit, she too had been raised in a home filled with physical and emotional abuse. She grew up in the border town of Brownsville, Texas, best known for being a military base and the port of call for steamboat fishermen who came in from South Padre Island.

She left home when she was sixteen to live with a man she was in a relationship with at the time. After they parted ways, she took on a variety of jobs to support herself. Even this wasn't enough to see to her needs, which is why she resorted to trading sexual favors with local fishermen for the food and money she needed to live.

In 1960, Grandma met the man who would end up being the father of her three youngest children, a fisherman who was on one of the South Padre boats that passed through Brownsville. He soon switched into construction jobs, and they married, which helped with her financial woes but otherwise was a terrible mistake. He was an alcoholic who beat her viciously when he was drunk. To escape the abuse and poverty, my grandmother drank too much herself.

By the time Julie was of school age, they were living in a two-bedroom wood-frame house in Brownsville. It's all boarded up now, but my grandmother's estate still owns it. To say their family was dysfunctional would be an understatement. Cramped together in this small space, there was nowhere for the children to escape the sight of their mother being beaten by her husband.

In time, Julie and her sisters became his targets. He would go out on drinking binges at night with my grandma's brother, hitting up the local bars or wild parties their friends were throwing. These binges would last for hours, the two men not returning home sometimes until the early morning, close to dawn, at which point they would touch and fondle Julie and her sisters. My mom was only about thirteen when these incidents began. It's hard to say whether my grandma knew about the abuse and was afraid to put a stop to it or she was so lost in her own mind that she was oblivious to what was happening right under her nose. Because she'd never been shown love by her own parents, her ability to nurture was further impaired by the hardships she'd experienced, thus repeating another cycle of painful intergenerational trauma with us, her children. Whatever the cause, under her watch, the cycle of abuse claimed another generation as its victims.

Because my grandma was both emotionally and physically unavailable, it often fell to Julie and her sisters to care for their youngest siblings as they grew. Despite this, they managed to stay in school and do well enough to hope for a better life than the one they'd been born into. Julie was a smart child and was determined to fulfill her dream of one day becoming a registered nurse. Though Grandma wouldn't let Julie see her birth father, Roberto had promised he would help pay for her schooling once she graduated from high school, which meant that dream might actually become a reality. But then she met my father her sophomore year, a young man named Peter, who was a grade above her. They quickly fell in love. While I don't know all the details of their relationship, I do know that in May 1967, as she came to the end of her eleventh-grade year, Julie was both still dating Peter and still a virgin.

That would change just a few weeks shy of summer break. Julie and Peter went on a date to the movies. After the film, he asked her to take a walk with him through a wooded area around a nearby lake—where he took her virginity. That's when I was conceived. It would be many years before I found out the full story of what happened that night.

Each summer when Julie was growing up, my grandmother would take the family and travel to faraway states like Michigan, Ohio, and Washington to work on farms as part of the migrant farmworker program. She'd use that money to help pay her bills throughout the year. The summer of 1967 was no different. A month after Julie lost her virginity to Peter, her family moved to a farm near Fremont, Ohio, to pick strawberries and other fruit all day long in the hot sun. She and my grandmother were not getting along, and two weeks after they arrived, my grandmother told her she could leave if she wouldn't listen. By then, Julie had befriended the deacon at a church in Fremont, and he and his wife offered her a job as nanny to their two children. After she confirmed with a local doctor she was pregnant, she was shattered. In an instant, her dream of becoming a registered nurse was gone. And she feared the wrath of my grandmother if she told her about the pregnancy. To help cover her maternity bills, Julie began working for a second family, who offered to pay her more to be their nanny and housekeeper, money she desperately needed to pay for the medical bills for the baby. The deacon's family had convinced her that giving me up for adoption was best, which was what Julie planned to do. She finally told my grandmother, who was still in Fremont, that November. Grandma begged her on hands and knees not to give me away. For some reason, that was enough to convince my mother.

I've always asked myself why my mother decided to keep me. I can't imagine she believed her own mother would be protective of me; Grandma had barely raised her own children, after all, and was the one who'd stood by and done nothing as they were molested. And I wonder too just what I was feeling as I floated there in my mother's womb. Could I feel that I'd been rejected even before I took my first breath? Was Little Nikki making her first appearance even then? I sometimes picture that rejection entering the very core of my soul, how it settled in and festered there, opening the doors to my future torments.

Around this same time, as the nights grew to a freezing chill in Fremont, a young man named Jack joined the congregation. He didn't have a Christian background but had come to the church in search of stability and guidance, much like my mother had. Julie and Jack started talking and quickly grew close. Jack pursued her with all he had, courting her with candy, cards, and small gifts. He was a womanizer, but he was so charming that he seemed like perfect husband material. Soon, they were legally married and renting a house of their own in Fremont. Jack had a stable job, so Julie quit her position as the deacon's nanny. The other family she worked for was so supportive of her, even helping her pay for her labor and maternity costs, something I have always been grateful for. I was born in January 1968, and less than a year after that, my mom was pregnant again with Jack's son, my half brother David.

My memories of Jack are sparse, so I'm not sure if there were warning signs of the abuse or if he was the kind of man who was well practiced at hiding his violent intentions. Regardless, the speed with which my mom went from living with the deacon to marrying Jack speaks to the fact that she was desperate for the love and affection she'd never gotten from her mother. I know Grandma prevented my mom from forming a relationship with her own father for many years, in much the same way my mom shut my biological father out of my life. Still, I wonder how things might have unfolded differently for my mom if she'd been shown love as a child. I can now see how that same lack of love affected my own relationships with men, driving me into multiple partnerships and marriages that were harmful for me. The wounds and shame of abuse weigh heavily on young shoulders, and that's a weight that doesn't get lifted easily. If not for those wounds, maybe Julie wouldn't have rushed into Jack's arms.

Maybe we both would have been spared the violence he inflicted upon us.

Every Monday morning, my mom would get ready for work, knowing we'd at least survived another week. She worked a lot while we were living in Ohio. On the days after Jack had beaten her, she would cover up her bruises with sweaters and head to her job as though nothing were wrong. Given how cold Ohio winters were, no one would question her long sleeves and other clothing choices. It was cold in our home too, but a different kind of cold, a bitter cold that cut deeper than the temperature—the kind of cold that comes from living with more pain than affection.

I don't think it's a coincidence that Jack found Julie when she was poor and had been abandoned by her own family; these were the exact traits that made her the perfect victim. Underprivileged women at all levels of society experience violence in their day-to-day lives at a far higher rate than others. That my mom had become isolated and separated from her family made it even easier for Jack to take advantage of her. And me.

His sexual abuse started when I was about two and a half years old. I was still too young for kindergarten, so I would stay home with Jack while Mom was at work; his shifts didn't start until the early afternoon. I remember one winter day, the snow falling heavily outside, when Jack called me up to their bedroom about an hour after Mom left. He asked me to jump up on the bed. When I did, he started to touch and kiss me; then he unbuckled his pants and exposed his penis, placing my hands on it. He told me we were playing a game, our special one. If I was good and played the role of his nice baby girl, he would love me. I was, of course, much too young to understand what was really happening. There was no way for me to know how horrible his behavior was or how much it would injure my soul for years and years to come. While I understood on some level that the game was wrong, I only knew that when we played it, he was nice to me, which felt like a kind of love. I craved any kind of warmth or kindness, and it was then, I think, I started learning that sex was a way to get the love and affection that was missing from my life.

Jack's sexual abuse continued for months. Sometimes he would call me into the bed to play our game. Other times he'd take me into the shower. I did whatever he told me to. I was afraid to tell my mom what Jack was doing to me while she was at work, much like she'd been afraid to tell her mom about her pregnancy, and for many of the same reasons, though I doubt I could have articulated that at the time. She'd already rejected me; if she knew what Jack was doing, that rejection would only get worse. This anxiety led me to begin wetting the bed. My mother made me wash my pajamas, underpants, and sheets as punishment.

As Jack's molestation intensified, so too did the domestic abuse he directed at my mom. He had begun whipping her with a leather belt, leaving marks on her arms and legs. Maybe that's why we finally made a run for it.

Though my mother was clashing a lot with my grand-mother, she was desperate to escape her abusive husband and so decided to return to Brownsville, Texas. I remember helping my mother pack a few bags and hiding them in an abandoned wrecked car on our property so we could leave without Jack finding out. She feared he would kill her if he knew what she was planning. I was terrified too, until we were able to flee in the dead of night while he was working. Our neighbors drove us to the bus station.

This was the spring of 1970, and I was not quite four years

old. I don't remember much about that bus ride from Ohio to Texas. All I know is it seemed long to me, so long that I probably drove my mother up the wall asking her when we'd arrive at my grandmother's house. It took us two days because we had to stop at gas stations frequently to change David's diapers. The ride must have felt longer still for Mom, with two small children in tow; new bruises on her arms and a cut lip, the latest marks of Jack's rage; and no guarantees she'd find the help she needed at the end of her journey. It's no wonder she'd been so careful with our escape. Mom was in a daze for most of that ride, but our troubles were far from over.

2

One Step Forward, One Step Back

Once we arrived in Brownsville, we stayed with my grand-mother, where my mom often remained secluded in her bed-room because of their rocky relationship. I remember being very lonely during this time, though I enjoyed watching my baby brother. We slept together on a rollaway cot. Not long after, my mother and grandmother's issues came to a head. My mom screamed at Grandma for keeping her from her own fa-ther for so many years, for setting a bad example by having so many children from different fathers, for not letting her have her father's last name. My mom was so furious, my grand-mother finally gave her the name and address for El Robles, one of her father's bars, and told her to go find him. Roberto Robles was a successful businessman who, in addition to two bars, owned some taxicabs, commercial tire shops, and real es-tate and was a partner in another bar, El Little Village.

Julie must have wondered what type of reception she'd get

from her father, as she'd only seen him sporadically when she was growing up, and it had usually been when her mother had gone to get money from him. My mom found him at El Robles. Though he wasn't very tall, he carried himself well and had an air of authority, no doubt due to his success as an entrepreneur. I don't have many memories of him, but I do vividly recall the first time we met. He was wearing a starched white shirt, black dress pants, and sunglasses, and he brought my brother and me some cotton candy. I felt an instant connection with him.

"What is your name, dear?" he asked me.

"Why?" I quickly responded. I was overjoyed with the thought of having a grandfather as a father figure, but I was very protective of my brother, so I swiftly added, "Do you like small children?"

"I love children," he said, winning me over.

"Sir, we do not have a family. What do I call you, sir?" I asked him shyly.

"I am your Grandpa Robles, and you have a family now," he replied.

Given that response, I literally jumped up and down with joy. I was even happier when he told us he wanted us to meet his family.

"You can all play in my home, and there is a nanny who will help you settle in," he said.

And so, for the first time, I got to experience a grandfather's love. His wife, Josefina, was equally gracious. She welcomed us into their home, filled with beautiful furniture and a refrigerator overflowing with food. They had a housekeeper, a nanny, and a lot of nice cars, among them a Lincoln Continental. Their children, several of them my mother's half siblings, were neatly dressed and well groomed. It was clear there was a lot of love in that house. It was my first glimpse of what a real family looks like.

My little brothers were one of the few bright spots in my early years. The second, Robert, was born that June of 1970. I nurtured them both with a true mother's love, as our mother lacked empathy. David, my little bundle of joy, was the cutest baby. He had brown eyes, chubby and jolly cheeks, and dark-brown hair. I remember I used to take him to my room and pretend I was his mother, giving him his bottle and trying to care for him. We were just eighteen months apart, so there wasn't much I could do for him; for instance, our mother had to change his diapers. But before our move, I had tried to keep him quiet on the weekends because if David made too much noise, Jack would tell my mom to "shut that kid up." I'd gently rock David back and forth in my arms to shush him if he whimpered or cried, hoping to keep Jack from getting angrier and hitting my mom or even hurting David.

Robert, named after my grandpa Roberto, was at first a clingy and colicky baby. Though he cried a lot, my mother would sometimes forbid me from carrying him, and I felt so anxious hearing his little cries go unanswered. I deeply desired to be protective of them both. I would become Little Nikki, physically shielding them from our mother's wrathful fists. She would spank us harshly and sometimes slapped David and Robert so hard that their mouths would bleed. Her favorite form of punishment, though, was emotional—and that type of pain would not go away the way the bruises did.

As a young girl, all I had witnessed until Grandpa and his wife came along was pain. Trauma. Sexual abuse. Rejection. I felt unloved and unworthy, with wounds that cut deep into my soul. Now, I had hope that things could be different. My grandfather quickly set us up in a rental home that was small but cozy, gave my mother a car, and hired a nanny-housekeeper, who could help my mom take care of us kids, though I wasn't thrilled about the way she treated my brothers. She was cruel, pushing their heads underwater while bathing them, pinching them, and pulling their hair. I told my mother what she was doing—I'd been acting as David's caretaker for as long as I could remember, and I was so protective of them both. However, my mother just told me to stop whining and help the nanny care for them.

But things were definitely better for my mom. My grandfather was even able to help her get back on track with her dream of becoming a nurse. There was no undoing the fact that she'd been forced to drop out of high school, but he helped her get into the Mercy Hospital nursing program. He put a lump sum into her account every month to help pay for our living expenses and part of her schooling, and a grant funded the other part. Her life's path had taken a long and painful detour, but thanks to my grandpa, she was back on a path toward a better future.

However, Jack didn't give up on my mom easily. He remembered that she'd always vowed to find her father; she'd even told Jack the name of the street her father's bar was on. So in May, just before Robert was born, he set out on that same long cross-country trek we'd made. I imagine he thought he would show how much he loved her and win her back. In reality, this meant he stalked us, a shadow of the violence mom had endured up north. He showed up at El Robles—since the bar was named after my grandfather, it hadn't been hard to figure it out—then followed him home. Josefina watched us on the days our nanny was off, so Jack followed us one day from Josefina and Roberto's home to our rental home after my mother picked us up. Mom had gone inside and left me to bring in David and Robert, so when I saw Jack exiting his car, I ran inside to alert her. She and Jack got into a terrible argument, and I ran to get help from our next-door neighbor. He yelled at Jack and told him he was calling the police. By the time they arrived, Jack was long gone. Another time, he followed my mother to the supermarket and snatched baby Robert from her grocery cart, yelling at her and calling her a whore, saying he had a gun. Mom told the supermarket manager, who called the police, while another employee told Jack to give Robert back because they were all witnesses and kidnapping was a felony that carried a jail sentence. Jack flew out the back exit door like a coward and was gone by the time the police arrived.

If my mom had been on her own, maybe his plan of intimidation would have worked. By this point, though, she had Grandpa watching over her. Once he found out Jack was bothering my mom, he took action to stop it. Grandpa confronted Jack when he showed up at the bar and demanded to see Julie and his sons, standing up to him the way a parent should defend their child. He told Jack that if he ever touched Julie again, he'd break Jack's bones. My mother finally filed a police report, and my grandfather hired a good attorney to help her divorce Jack. He had no choice but to slink off back to Ohio, his tail between his legs. Once their divorce was finalized in late 1971, he was out of our lives for good.

Moving back to Texas—and getting away from Jack— helped my mom find so many of the things she'd been deprived of throughout her childhood. She finally had a parent she could lean on, for one thing. Thanks to her dad's help, she'd escaped her abuser and was working in a hospital, back on track with the life she'd dreamed of living. That's not to say everything was perfect. She was still tormented by the abuse

she'd suffered long after the divorce was finalized, just like I
carried the scars of Jack's abuse into my adulthood. Things
were better, but, as much as I wished otherwise, it was too
late to erase the damage that had already been done. Still, on a
day-to-day level, our lives were calmer and happier than they'd
ever been in Ohio. And at least my brothers were spared much
of the violence that had shaped my early life. I did my best to
make sure of that.

***

Julie often worked the graveyard shift at the emergency room,
which is how she met my future stepfather, whom I called
Daddy Lou. One night in September 1971, she finished up dis-
pensing medication in the intensive care unit and was crossing
the hallway that led to the emergency room when her supervisor asked her to assist with victims of a terrible car accident.
One of them had just arrived. He was covered with blood and
looked to be on the verge of death. They quickly took him
down the hall for emergency surgery. Off to her right, she saw
hospital personnel gathered around another stretcher, franti-
cally trying to resuscitate a young woman, to no avail. She was
already dead. Julie noticed a lump under the sheet beside the
young woman but didn't know what it was.

Their car had been hit by a drunk driver as they were coming home from a family gathering. Daddy Lou had also been
drinking before he'd gotten into the car with his wife and two-
month-old daughter around two in the morning, and maybe he
could have responded more quickly if he hadn't had anything
to drink, but the other driver was the one at fault. His wife had
been holding the baby in her lap, and both had been ejected

from the car on impact and died instantly; the baby's tiny body had been the bundle my mom had seen on that stretcher.

Daddy Lou's injuries were severe, but he survived and was moved into the ICU to recover. He would end up staying in the hospital for about three weeks, and my mom was one of the nurse's aides who cared for him. She found herself drawn to this patient in room A477. He had such a kind, gentle spirit. I think she felt for his pain too. My mom had endured so much violence and tragedy already in her life, and her heart went out to this man who'd had his entire world blown apart in one awful moment.

She saw him sobbing desperately once, trying to rip out his IV to go find his beloved young wife and infant daughter. Other times he just cried and asked for them. The doctors wanted to keep him calm, so they kept him sedated with morphine. When he was finally well enough, his daughter's godparents gave him the devastating news of the deaths of his wife and child. He wept unconsolably, for the loss of both of them their loss and the pain of thinking he was responsible for their deaths. Though the accident had not been his fault, he still felt immense guilt for it.

Even in the most difficult life, there are moments of grace, and this was true for my mom. I believe God put her on that shift, in that hospital, bringing Daddy Lou into her life and us into his. Daddy Lou never forgave himself for the accident that killed his first wife and baby daughter. I think he saw my mom, brothers, and me as a way to get a second chance at raising a family, and from the beginning, he brought a lot of love into our household. It was in Daddy Lou that I would get my first real father figure, the only one whom I ever felt right calling my dad. I believe God spared Daddy Lou for a reason: to care

for a family that desperately needed both love and protection.
Daddy Lou had lost a family, but there was another one waiting for him. He loved us unconditionally, as though we were
his own. And I'm so thankful he was in our life, especially considering what was soon to come.

Mom and Daddy Lou married just three months after
they met, in a simple ceremony at the courthouse with no
guests. My brothers and I weren't even allowed to attend. My
earliest vivid memories of being with Daddy Lou come from
that first Christmas he spent with us. He was five feet, eight
inches tall, with jet-black hair, green eyes, and a husky build,
and he worked in a local cold storage warehouse. I remember
him holding me up so I could place the angel on top of the
Christmas tree. He bought us presents. I got a doll and a play
dish set, while my brothers got Tonka-type toy trucks. He also
bought us a beautiful red swing set for the backyard.

"Are you going to love us and never leave us?" I asked him.

"My little girl, from today on, you will be my daughter, and
I will be a father to you and your brothers," he told me. "I will
love your mom as long as I live."

It's a promise he kept.

More than the presents, though, I think it was Daddy
Lou's love that made Christmas feel so special that year. When
Daddy Lou looked at me, I think he saw the daughter he'd lost,
pouring into me all the affection he'd never have a chance to
give to her. This paternal love was exactly what I'd been missing in my life.

Unfortunately, my mom wasn't as lucky as I was in that
respect. Her rekindled connection with her own father never
really had a chance to blossom. The same month that Mom
married Daddy Lou, less than a year after we first arrived,
my grandpa was shot at El Robles. He survived but developed

gangrene after the surgery and died a month later. He was just forty-three years old. Mom was assigned to his case as one of his medication aides, and his death was another blow to her already fractured soul, as it was to mine. As one of my mom's friends once said, it was like there was a curse on our family; just when it seemed like one of us was about to escape the generational violence, something would strike to keep us trapped in it.

Thankfully, though, my mother wasn't left completely on her own. We could no longer afford the nanny, but she still had Daddy Lou, and she had Josefina to help her with childcare, especially at night and on the weekends, when she and Daddy Lou both worked. We were allowed to stay in the rental home, but Mom needed a second job, as a waitress, to pay the rent. During the day, she still worked at the hospital as a nurse's aide and trained to become a licensed vocational nurse. In those days, becoming a nurse's aide didn't require much formal education and relied more on hands-on experience. Her dreams of becoming a registered nurse had died with my grandfather. She simply couldn't afford to do it anymore, not even with Daddy Lou's salary to help pay the bills. A few months into their marriage, he asked her to put aside her career aspirations entirely and stay home to care for us kids, so that's what she did.

My grandpa's death took Mom to a dark place, one that she didn't truly begin to emerge from for more than a year. She isolated herself instead of reaching out for help, help that is so important for healing and survival. When she did speak, she'd have violent outbursts, which she directed at me. For the sake of protecting my brothers, I'd become accustomed to being the target. Despite how young we all were, I saw them as being so much more defenseless than I was. So I tried to handle things on my own, with Little Nikki's help. As Little Nikki, I would try to divert her outbursts from my brothers as much as I could. Maybe that's why I began wetting the bed again, something that had stopped when we'd first arrived in Brownsville. Or maybe the bed-wetting had been triggered by my grandfather's death and the combined burdens of loneliness and the heavy responsibilities I bore at such a young age. Whatever the reason, it enraged my mother, and she'd check my sheets daily, sometimes pushing my head down so I could smell the sheets myself. She made me wash the dirty sheets and clothing I was wearing. The bed-wetting continued off and on until I was ten and Daddy Lou convinced my mother to take me to a doctor, who prescribed me Tofranil for anxiety. After that, the bed-wetting became less frequent.

It's taken me many years of counseling to understand I shouldn't have had to take on those roles as a child, that having those responsibilities led to me living daily with both panic and anxiety, which I still carry with me today. All were related to this role reversal of parent and child and left me deeply emotionally scarred, as I had to become Little Nikki almost all the time to try to both parent my brothers and shield them from our mother's verbal and physical abuse. These compulsions that started in my childhood became exacerbated in adulthood. I had thought I owed my brothers the care I gave them, but I didn't. That had been my mom's job, not mine, and she'd failed miserably at it. How could they ever have understood that I suffered chronic stress and anxiety because there was never a reliable adult around? Even now, I still need to wash my clothes daily, a leftover habit from my childhood when I had to clean my urine-soaked sheets.

***

In early 1973, my mom found out she was expecting her first child with Daddy Lou, to be born in October. And it would be a boy! I was so happy. I loved mothering David and Robert, and I was looking forward to helping care for the new little one on the way. I couldn't wait to hold him in my arms.

It was a difficult pregnancy for my mother. She had gestational high blood pressure and had to rest as much as she could, so I did what I could to help her out. I'd make peanut butter and jelly sandwiches for my brothers and bring her warm water with Epsom salts to soak her swollen feet. The days before my newest baby brother made his grand entrance passed quickly. My aunts threw her a baby shower, and I helped her put away all the gifts for him.

I also helped Mom pack the day before she went to the hospital for her C-section, which her doctor had scheduled because it was a high-risk pregnancy and the baby was so big. I filled her suitcase with the new baby clothes (including socks and onesies), a blanket, and bottles from the baby shower, marveling at how precious the little baby blankets were. Once Mom left for the hospital, a housekeeper stayed with us while Daddy Lou was at work, though I helped with feeding, bathing, and caring for my brothers. The birth went well, but my mom stayed at the hospital for a few days. I was desperate to meet Arthur, my new baby brother, so Daddy Lou and my aunt Amy, my mother's half sister, took me to meet him. I held Art in my arms, all ten pounds of him, then hugged him close to my body and kissed him on the forehead. His little face was so angelic. I soaked up every detail—his little fingers, his hair, his eyes. It was truly a special moment.

As much as I loved my new family, it couldn't erase all the scars and trauma from my early years with Jack in Ohio. It felt like there was a shadow of fear and shame that followed me everywhere I went. I became painfully shy and had trouble building the self-esteem I needed to interact with other kids. I craved love and desperately wanted my mother's approval. My mom was still dealing with the lingering effects of the trauma and abuse she'd suffered too. The abuse by her uncle and step-father, followed by the domestic violence she'd endured during her marriage to Jack—all that pain was still there, and I don't think she ever learned a way to escape it. These demons made her a difficult person to live with, especially for me as the most common target of her pent-up anger and resentment.

That's not to say Daddy Lou didn't have issues too. He was an alcoholic and would often drink heavily, I think partially as a way to help him deal with the grief from the accident that had brought him and my mom together. He preferred tequila and other types of hard liquor and would often drink full bottles when he was home, especially during Thanksgiving and Christmas, which were tough holidays for him as he remembered his lost family. He was a good man at his core, though, with a kind heart. He did his best to protect me and my brothers from the brunt of our mother's rage. He brought love into our house and made it feel like a home, not just a place I so desperately wanted to escape. For the first time, I felt like I had a family, and I couldn't have asked for a better father than Daddy Lou.

***

After I turned six, I began attending first grade at Garden Park Elementary School. My teachers saw how shy I was and did what they could to bring me out of my shell. I especially remember one of my teachers, Mrs. Freeman. She never gave up on me, encouraging me to take part in group activities in the classroom, though I never could muster up the courage to participate. When I did speak up in class, it was Little Nikki's voice that would come out, the voice of the scared, small child inside me. She was such a sweet girl, but she didn't have the power to fully express her needs. Mrs. Freeman was one of the few teachers who saw the pain behind my shyness and reached out, giving me the approval I sought from all the adult figures in my life. It was hard for me to talk in class, but I would often volunteer my time to do chores around the classroom, mostly as a way to get that little bit of attention and approval I didn't get from my mom at home. Sometimes I would retreat into fantasy and daydream that one of my teachers had adopted me, usually Mrs. Freeman. In these dreams, I was whisked away to a stable home where there was no anger or abuse, under the care of a mother who was loving and kind. Even Daddy Lou's love wasn't enough to make up for my mother's failings.

I was a kind child, inclined toward people-pleasing even at a very young age, but my shyness still made it very difficult for me to make friends. One of my mom's friends had a daughter around my age, and we'd walk home from school together, but it was hard for me to form a relationship any deeper than this with anyone my own age. For one thing, I couldn't exactly bring them home to play. Around this age, I again became a caretaker for my younger brothers, charged with doing the household chores after school while my mom watched TV in her room. I loved my brothers with all my heart and wanted to spare them the pain and anger I suffered under. This was when I developed an obsessive-compulsive need to keep everything clean, whether it was washing the dishes or keeping up with the laundry. I think I was hoping that if everything in the house was perfect, my mom wouldn't yell at us or punish us. Honestly, her hateful words cut far deeper than being beaten with a belt, her physical punishment of choice when she lashed out. I was a nervous wreck at home, always walking on eggshells and constantly on edge; her anger was unpredictable, and I was too young to see my actions weren't the cause of it.

My mother was eventually diagnosed with bipolar disorder and borderline personality disorder. During her manic periods, she'd take us kids out shopping, buying us treats from the dollar store or local shops. Yet when she was in a downward swing, her depression was intense. She'd spend days crying, overwhelmed by her feelings of sadness until those feelings compounded into a frightening rage that she'd unleash on me or Daddy Lou. All the negativity and vitriol molded my mind, destroying my fledgling attempts at building self-esteem. Daddy Lou's love couldn't do much to help in the face of that kind of onslaught.

Little Nikki did whatever she could to keep the peace in our home, though it was never an easy task.

***

Daddy Lou had a large family, and they welcomed us into it. Most of his family members were very kind to us; I especially remember that my step-grandma was a sweet woman and that I enjoyed the time I got to spend with her. My step-grandpa was a merchant in Mexico who sold small electronics and firearms. Every few months, he would travel north to Texas to buy the electronics he took back to Mexico and sold.

My step-grandpa started staying with us when he was in town. Mom and Daddy Lou would often leave him to watch us kids while they went out to dance halls and parties. While they were gone, he would molest me. It started when I was six years old and continued until I was eight. I don't recall there ever being penetration, unless I've blocked out those memories completely, but he touched me sexually and with enough intensity that I experienced my first orgasm when I was about seven. The good feelings that would happen in my body when he stimulated me were too confusing for me to deal with, and I couldn't seem to stop them, no matter how hard I fought them down. And so it was that Little Nikki would emerge, a small, shy girl starved for love and attention. I recall feeling protected and wanted, but it's clear that I was confusing the sexual contact for the love Little Nikki desperately needed.

The shame that came with these feelings of pleasure was the most damaging part of the experience for my young mind. Eventually, I internalized the shame and fear; if this was making me feel good, clearly I was the one who was wrong. It was this shame that kept me from ever talking about the abuse with my parents, or with anyone, until I was much older. I was a child, and I had absolutely no control over how I was living. I remember wanting to be loved so badly I could not say no to my abusers. It was easy for them to groom me, as any time I was shown kindness, Little Nikki became eager to please. But afterward, she would retreat, shy, full of shame, and so sad.

No mother in her right mind should leave her daughter in the care of an older man she hardly knows. But then, my mom had never been very protective of me, negligent even when she was at her best, and she certainly wasn't in her right mind most of the time. It was a generational neglect; no one had been there to protect her as a child, and that was the only kind of parenting she ever knew. Maybe she didn't realize how much I needed her guidance; maybe she just didn't know how to provide it. Whatever the reason, the cycle of abuse was perpetuated yet again.

In the summer of 1974, when I was six going on seven, my

step-grandpa sent his son Uncle Jesus to stay with us. Jesus also lived in Mexico, coming to Texas for temporary work for short periods, usually between three and six months, before heading back home. This was the start of a new miserable chapter in my young life. Jesus too was a sexual predator, and I soon became a victim of his attentions. Just like my step-grandpa, Jesus would offer to watch us kids, molesting me while my parents were out of the house. I never told anyone about the abuse because I was afraid Daddy Lou would confront them violently.

While this abuse was happening, my mom's mental health continued to decline. Her emotions were mercurial, their shifts unpredictable, and her parenting style was completely dependent on her moods. It didn't take much to trigger an angry outburst from her. Since I couldn't control her, I poured my energy into controlling everything else in my surroundings. I washed my brothers' clothes in the old wringer washer we had, my small, skinny arms barely able to spin the clothes through the rollers. I cooked their meals, simple ones like macaroni and cheese with hot dogs. When Mom was in one of her depressive states, there were times where she would not come out of her room for days, so I would bring her canned Campbell's soup and crackers. Chicken with rice was her favorite. The more overcontrolling and anxious she was, the more hypercritical of myself I became. As soon as I came home from school, I would rush straight to my mom to ask what chores needed to be done, still hoping that if I was obedient and did everything she asked, she would finally give me the love I so desperately craved. I did the same at school, always volunteering to help the teachers, eager for their acknowledgment. Ironically, I often got more gratitude at school than at home. I remember once a teacher bought me a cookie as a thanks for something I'd helped out with. It seems like a small gesture, but at the time, it made my day just to get a taste of approval from an adult in my life.

One of the few bright spots in my early childhood was my aunt Amy, who also lived in Brownsville. After we moved back from Ohio, she became a mother figure to me, and in many of my best memories, she is there, smiling and appreciating me. She taught me how to bake, wash dishes, and set up tables for get-togethers, all of which helped me raise my brothers. I have fond memories of when she hosted family potluck barbecues on an open field at Fort Brown in Brownsville. My aunts would bring their favorite casseroles and other dishes as well as homemade cookies and cupcakes. Everyone would gather, and it was always a day of laughter and feeling like a real family.

Another memory that stands out is of Easter when I was eight years old. I so wanted to wear a white dress. I'd always wanted to wear one, though I don't know why. Maybe it's because I wished I were a princess. I admit I was a hopeless dreamer; it helped me escape what was going on in my real life. That year, Aunt Amy surprised me with a beautiful white Easter dress with pastel-colored embroidered flowers on it and a corsage she'd made herself. I was so thrilled I proudly wore it to Easter Mass that day. Church was important to Daddy Lou, who'd been raised Catholic, and he did his best to instill some sort of religious faith in us. Easter was one of the few times my mother agreed to go too.

Afterward, I changed into shorts and a T-shirt for the family picnic and had a blast with my younger cousins. Aunt Amy put together an Easter egg hunt and always had some golden eggs she filled with dollar bills and candy. I don't know why, but I always seemed to be the one that found the golden eggs each year, perhaps a little bit of grace and divine intervention for all that I had already been through at such a young age.

Another great memory is from when I turned eleven and my mother let Aunt Amy host a birthday celebration for me at her home. She took my cousins and me shopping and bought me some shoes, a dress, nail polish, hair combs, and things like that. Then she took us out to eat at Luby's, a chain of cafeteria-style restaurants, one of my favorites. She even bought me a cake. It was the best birthday ever. I don't know what I would have done without Aunt Amy in my life when I was a child.

***

As Daddy Lou's big family was fervent about following their Catholic beliefs, there was always some kind of religious imagery in the house, like a crucifix on the wall or a statue of the Virgin Mary. There are times I think they protected me from my mother's wrath.

My mother had an array of different punishments for me and my brothers. While her go-to was to beat us with a belt, other abuses were both psychological and physical; one of her favorites was to have us kneel in a dark closet. Sometimes she used Daddy Lou as an agent, sending him to carry out our punishments, though he protected us from violence whenever he could. He would have us kneel in the closet as a less painful alternative to the belt. He was probably just as afraid of my mom's mood swings as we were and was just as often a target of her vitriol.

My brothers and I learned to hide our bruises. I would try to take the beatings for my brothers, blocking my mother when she swung that thick leather belt at them, but she sometimes still got them. She used to hit us on our arms, legs, and backs with that belt. I remember once in sixth grade I was supposed to wear shorts during PE class. The coach that year was a harsh woman, very much a stickler for the rules, and was not very pleased when I refused to change out of my long pants. It was my nature to do what the teachers asked, but I was more scared of what my mom would do if the coach saw the bruises from her latest session with the belt.

Most kids get help from their parents when they need to cope with pain or tragedy. Since I couldn't get that, I started to develop my own coping mechanisms. As much as I wanted love from my mom, I also wanted an escape from her constant blame. With no safe space to go to in my home, I created one inside my mind with Little Nikki. I told myself over and over that the abuse had never happened, creating an alternate reality where we were a normal, happy family and all those awful things had happened to another girl, Little Nikki, who was separate from me. I imagined I was the child of my favorite teacher, who was a sympathetic ear for me when I'd had a particularly bad run-in with my mother. I wished for this to be true so much, and for so long, that these comforting delusions overtook my memories, forcing my experiences down deep into my mind, where I could pretend they didn't exist. Splitting myself into separate identities was the only way my mind could put some distance between myself and those painful memories.

These mental barriers helped me keep going on a day-by-day basis, but they couldn't protect me from myself. I so wanted to be loved by someone, anyone, and being molested at such a young age taught me that sex was a way to get a kind of positive attention. I started to take an interest in boys when I was about eleven—and the wrong kind all too often. In sixth grade at age twelve, I also had my first boyfriend and first kiss. Unfortunately, it happened at school, and we were caught in the act by that same PE teacher, who had already decided I was disobedient. She suspended both of us and planned to send us home. There wasn't a home phone line in our house at that time, so the school's counselor called our landlord, who lived in the home next door. That might have been part of what made my mom so angry—not just that I'd gotten into trouble but that she'd heard about it from a neighbor, that I'd embarrassed her.

I could tell my mom was furious as soon as she got to the school. Once we were home, she told me to kneel down in her room, facing the crucifix that was hanging on the wall. She came in and told me to ask Jesus to forgive me, then shamed me for kissing a boy, spewing out a venomous stream of hateful speech. The beating that followed was one of the worst she ever gave me. She seemed determined to make sure I remembered my first kiss not as a cute and innocent milestone but as a source of anxiety and fear. It was only kissing, but instead of seeing that as the call for help it was, my mom's response to my budding promiscuity was to shame and chastise me, which ironically would only go on to drive me away and into the arms of any boy who'd have me.

As I knelt there, staring at Christ hanging on the cross, I saw his pain reflected back at me. I thought about what he'd endured, not just beatings but a crucifixion. I was all too familiar with sorrow in my young life, and imagining his, I thought of how much his love for humanity must have burned that he would endure that kind of torment just to save us from our sins. There, on my knees, with my mother's blows raining down on me, I said his name: "Jesus."

Suddenly, her hand froze in midair. She turned, in a daze, and left the room. It was like her inner demons had been scared off by the power of Jesus's name once I had spoken it aloud. The welts from her blows were searing, but more than the pain, I remember this moment as my first personal encounter with the living Jesus. I had called on him, and he had answered. I didn't have the power to escape my mother yet, but at least I wasn't alone in my suffering. There was a higher source of grace sustaining my life then, as it still does now.

3

The Frying Pan to the Fire

My mother wasn't always cruel to me. She had moments where she was incredibly kind, even maternal. For my twelfth birthday, she gathered some of my best friends and held a birthday party for me. She prepared some sandwiches, punch, and homemade cookies and even bought me a cake.

With Daddy Lou, it was much less complicated. I knew he loved me and my brothers unconditionally. From the moment he came into our lives, he treated all of us like his own children, doing everything he could to keep us safe and happy. This included providing for us financially, though that was hard to do in Brownsville. It was a small town back then, and Daddy Lou worked as a physical laborer, as he did not have the skills or experience necessary to be hired into one of the few high-paying jobs that were available. He realized that if he wanted to build a better life for his family, he would need to look for opportunities elsewhere. His brother Jesus was living in the United States full time by this point, and Jesus and his wife, Amber, lived outside of Dallas, Texas, in a town called Garland. Having family in the city meant we'd have a place to stay while we got settled, and the city itself had a thriving economy with a lot of employment options for a hard worker like Daddy Lou. And so, in 1981, he and Mom packed up our few belongings in the family station wagon and made the eight-hour drive north.

I was thirteen when we moved to Garland. It was the start of summer, and I had just finished my sixth-grade year. It had been six years since Jesus had stayed with us in Brownsville— six years since he'd fondled me while my parents were out of the house. I was uneasy about living under the same roof as him again, but I kept those anxious feelings buried and pretended that Uncle Jesus had done those things to another girl. Little Nikki took the brunt of this psychological damage as I embraced that fantasy. It was the only way I could survive living in close quarters with him again.

Uncle Jesus's home in Garland was a small wood-frame house with just two bedrooms. Needless to say, it was a bit crowded with my aunt and uncle, my parents, and me and my three brothers all living there together. The adults took the two bedrooms, while my three brothers and I squeezed together in the living room. I usually slept on the sofa, and my brothers slept on blankets on the floor. We had lived in small homes before, though, and in every other respect, the move was turning out to be a great thing for all of us. Daddy Lou found a construction job quickly, and my mom was able to find work as an assembly-line worker at a local manufacturing plant thanks to a recommendation from Amber. Something had changed with the move. There was a new glow to my mom, a joy in her face I had never seen before. It was almost as if she were a different person here in Garland, like she'd left the angry, bitter woman I'd known back in Brownsville.

Before the move, we'd had to live frugally, squeezing the last drop out of every penny of Daddy Lou's paycheck. He always made sure we had all the necessities, and we never went hungry, but there wasn't a lot of money left over for extras like trendy clothes. Now, though, not only was Daddy Lou making more, but Mom was bringing in an income—and this influx of spending money came at the perfect time, considering I'd just become a teenager. I would be starting my seventh-grade year in style, with a new wardrobe of nice pants, shirts, and shoes and even a few pairs of shorts for getting through the hot Garland summer.

It wasn't just getting nice new things that made the summer of 1981 one of the happiest I can remember. Mom's good mood sustained itself well after the move. Her judgment, criticism, and negativity—they had all miraculously vanished along with her anger. She walked around the house now like she was in her own world, completely content. Daddy Lou seemed happier too. I'm sure he was just as relieved at my mom's sudden mental shift as we kids were, and it probably took some stress off, knowing he wasn't the only one responsible for our livelihoods anymore. On his days off, he would relax with Jesus, listening to music and drinking a few beers. For years, I'd been pretending that I lived in a normal family, but that summer we actually were one.

Jesus and Amber didn't have kids of their own, but their home was in a neighborhood with a lot of families. I got to know a few of the local girls and found out some of them would be going to the same middle school as me when I started in the fall. During the first part of the summer, we played together around the neighborhood and made plans for the upcoming school year. I became fast friends with a girl named Paula, who lived two doors down from us. We'd hang out at her house sometimes, and her family was always nice to me whenever I stopped by. They lived modestly, but there was a lot of love in that house. I could see it whenever I watched her mom and dad talk to each other and in the way they spoke to Paula and her siblings. It was the kind of loving, supportive family I'd always craved. I don't think that alone was the reason I liked Paula, but I certainly enjoyed every chance I got to spend time in her home.

***

Shortly after our move, Amber's nephew Cesar also came to live with us. Like Daddy Lou, Cesar had come to Dallas in search of better work, hoping to escape the rough life he'd lived in Mexico. I was drawn to Cesar immediately. At nineteen, he was six years older than me, with a magnetic personality and kindly demeanor, and I quickly started seeing him as my knight in shining armor. I related to him too. Like me, Cesar was a victim of abuse. He'd watched his father beat his mother from the time he was young, and he had suffered beatings as well. His mom had taken him and escaped from his father a few years before, and she'd remarried to a hardworking man who treated her well. Even so, Cesar carried a lot of anger because of his early trauma. Later, I'd be able to recognize the demons that boiled inside him.

When my mom came home from work and spoke down to me, Cesar couldn't help but hear and take notice. When we talked, Cesar listened with his full undivided attention, offering sympathy and acceptance instead of criticism and rejection. I was still doing a lot of the work to take care of my brothers, and Cesar stepped in to help there too. He knew what it felt like to be responsible for family. He had a younger sister back in Mexico and wanted to send money home to her and his mom now that he was working.

In my thirteen-year-old eyes, Cesar was perfect. I would daydream about him, innocent fantasies of covert kisses and idyllic young love. He clearly had feelings for me too, and his affection made me feel like a princess. The only man who'd ever cared for me before was Daddy Lou, and as much as he tried to protect us from my mother, he couldn't. Cesar wasn't under my mom's control, though. He could protect me even from her, and that made him the escape route I needed.

Cesar was also a construction worker, which meant he could only work when the weather cooperated, so he would stay home when it rained. I spent that summer watching my younger brothers, who by this point looked to me for guidance and care more than they looked to my mother. On one hot, rainy summer day, when all the other adults were out of the house, Cesar suggested that we sneak away to get a little bit of time alone. There was a wooded area behind the house that led into a nice park, and this seemed like the perfect place to go. I told my brothers to stay put and that if anyone asked, they should tell them I went to my friend Paula's house.

This done, I raced to the back of the house to meet Cesar. I was infatuated with him, eager to be loved. That day in the park, I reached out my hand, and he took it. A bond formed between us. Cesar asked me if I'd ever kissed a boy, and I told him about the incident from the previous school year, when the PE coach had caught me with a boy under the bleachers. I had never talked to anyone about my mom's abuse before, but now the whole story came out. I told him how she'd made me kneel in front of the crucifix, and how I'd called out to Jesus while she'd beaten me with her belt. The entire time, Cesar held my hand, listening attentively, without judgment. When I finished, he wiped the tears from my cheeks and kissed my closed lips. This was a different kiss from the one under the bleachers. I was in love with Cesar, or at least the parts of him I knew. I hadn't yet seen the demons lurking in his soul.

For the rest of the summer, Cesar and I took any opportunity we had to sneak away and spend time together. Mostly we just held hands and hugged, and we never got more physical than kissing. It felt so innocent in those early days. We figured out one way to be together by asking Amber to take us with her to church. Amber quickly saw what was going on between me and Cesar and expressed her disapproval, but she at least didn't tell my mom about it. I think she was a bit afraid of what my mom would do if she found out, to be honest. Even though her moods had been more stable since the move, she could still be an angry and difficult woman, and I wasn't the only one who was perpetually overcautious around her.

Most days in the summer of 1981, my mom, Daddy Lou, and my aunt and uncle would work until the early evening. Cesar was gone most of the day when there were construction jobs to be had too, leaving me alone with my brothers and my own thoughts. Anxiety had been my constant companion for years, and it would assert itself the most whenever I was left alone, making me restless and eager for something to distract my mind. Of the adults in the household, Uncle Jesus was the one who'd come home first, usually two or three hours before any of the others. At first, we would just talk and visit, developing a friendship, but soon enough Jesus started showing me the same attention he had when I was a child in Brownsville. Jesus fondled me in the house while my brothers were watching TV in the other room or playing outside with their friends.

There was never any penetration, but it was sustained sexual contact, enough to bring me to orgasm.

The renewed sexual abuse added another layer of confusion to my already muddled psyche. Just like when I was a child, I felt immense shame over the good feelings that happened from being touched by men, especially as my relationship with Cesar started to get more physical. I was blossoming out of childhood, becoming a young woman and gaining a new awareness of my body. I started wearing shorter shorts and trying to use makeup, often bought for me by Cesar; I learned that I could charm my way into getting him to buy me what I wanted.

I was just going through puberty and learning my place in the world. I wasn't fully aware of the dangerous lesson that this sexual attention was instilling in me, but I internalized it nonetheless. I learned to look toward men for affirmation, believing more with every passing day that Cesar was my savior, the person who would take care of me and guide me to something better. No one had ever taught me to make decisions for myself, find my own self-worth, or take agency over my own life. Most of my life I'd been talked over by my mom, told how I should act and think. This had left me gullible, easily influenced, and afraid of standing up for myself. In short, the ideal target for abuse. I didn't realize all the little ways I was emulating the behaviors of the other women in my family.

As the summer faded into fall, the reality hit that I would soon be starting seventh grade. That would mean no more free time to see Cesar, no more sneaking off behind the house on rainy days. I told him our relationship would have to go on hold, a thought that tore me up inside. I knew I should go to school and get an education, but a part of me burned to be with Cesar. I hated that I felt I had to choose one or the other. The back-to-school shopping and preparations of early September passed by in a blur, my thoughts always dwelling on the question of what I should do.

Then, the week before school started, Cesar proposed to me. He found me in the hallway of our church, where I was going to Sunday youth school. He had planned everything: he said he'd been saving up money and had enough to give us a better future, promising me a full wedding ceremony complete with a white dress. He told me he had a car waiting outside to take us away, that this was our chance to make our escape. As far as I could see, this was the best thing that could have happened. Finally, after all these years, I'd be getting away from my mother. That I would be with Cesar—my Prince Charming—made it all the better.

We spent the night at the apartment of one of Cesar's friends. The next morning, we heard loud banging on the front door and knew it was the police looking for us. Since I was still a minor and Cesar was nineteen, he could face jail time if my mom decided to press charges against him—which I knew she would if she had the chance. Cesar and I hadn't had sex, and we'd agreed we wouldn't until we were legally married, but that wouldn't stop my mother from making the allegation. I didn't want to go home and face her; I was afraid of the punishment she'd dole out against me and even more afraid that Cesar would go to jail and I'd lose my protector.

Cesar's friend tried to hide us from the police, but they wouldn't leave. Eventually, Cesar convinced me I'd have to go with the officers. They told me that my mom and Daddy Lou were waiting to pick me up at the police station. Cesar was loaded into a separate police car, I assumed to be put in a cell while the investigation happened. As a last resort, I told the police officer during the ride to the station that my mom was abusive. I told him about her beating me and that I lived in constant fear of her wild moods and angry outbursts. I told the officer I'd go anywhere else willingly—even Cesar. It was clear I did not know any better at that time. I was just a child.

I didn't hear the conversation that happened between my mother and the investigator when we reached the police station. What I do know is that my mother dropped the charges against Cesar, and he was set free. I left the police station with my mom and Daddy Lou, and Daddy Lou started to drive us home. We hadn't gotten far when she told him to stop, turning around to look me in the eye. "You left with him," she said. "Now, you live with him. I want nothing to do with you. You're dead to me."

They were words meant to wound, but they made me happier than anything she'd said to me before. I had her permission to live with Cesar; as far as I was concerned, she'd just set me free.

***

Cesar didn't go back to Jesus and Amber's house after our encounter with the police; instead, he stayed with his aunt Mary and uncle Joey. Joey was another of Daddy Lou's brothers, and he and his wife had a sixteen-year-old daughter of their own, Jenny. When Daddy Lou dropped me off at their house, Cesar was so excited to be reunited with me that he ran outside when our car pulled up and picked me up in his arms.

As he'd promised, Cesar started preparing for our wedding. Jenny was also engaged and in the midst of wedding planning too. We decided to make it a double wedding, held in the same church Cesar and I had gone to with Amber over the summer. He even bought me a dress, snow white and sequined with faux diamonds and pearls, and a pair of satin shoes to match. When I tried the dress on, I felt like I was in a fairy tale; I couldn't remember ever having been so happy.

Unfortunately, since I was a minor, I couldn't get married without my mother's permission. Even though she'd allowed me to go live with Cesar, she refused to sign the consent form that would let us legally wed. Joey and Mary tried to reason with her, but she wouldn't relent. She was too bitter, still angry with me for rejecting her in favor of Cesar. Since she refused to sign the marriage license, we had no choice but to cancel the wedding. I wept bitterly that night. For weeks after, I'd put on my fairy-tale dress and satin shoes and walk through the house, dreaming of the wedding that I would never have, furious with my mom for denying me that happiness. Cesar changed after that too. He'd promised me a wedding, and now that wasn't possible, and this sent him spiraling into bouts of depression. He started drinking more and became very possessive, exhibiting signs of jealousy he hadn't shown before.

Cesar and I lived with Joey and Mary for about a year. Even though we couldn't get married in society's eyes, I wanted to be his wife, so I took on the duties of a homemaker instead of going back to school. I didn't see my family during this time and didn't realize how much my absence was affecting Daddy Lou. I know he loved me like a daughter, even though my mom's domineering nature sometimes prevented him from showing it like he wanted to. I imagine it was at his urging that they went to see Cesar at his workplace. They weren't living with Jesus and Amber anymore, having instead moved into a two-bedroom apartment, and they wanted me and Cesar to come live with them and share the expenses. I was torn on what to do. As much as I still feared my mom, I also missed my brothers and Daddy Lou. In the end, that won out over my fear, and we moved in with them.

I fell naturally back into being a caretaker for my younger brothers. If anything, it felt even more right now that I'd settled into a homemaker role with Cesar. It was nice to be reunited with them. I'd missed my brothers and Daddy Lou a lot while I'd been gone, and it was clear they'd missed me too. We weren't a traditional family unit, but we were happy in our own way, though this isn't to say it was entirely peaceful. I'd finally discovered the reason for my mother's good moods: she was cheating on Daddy Lou with a coworker, and by this point, Daddy Lou had started to suspect what was going on.

I imagine he was hesitant to confront her about it at first, considering how difficult she could be even at the best of times. By the time I moved back in with them, the affair had been going on for more than a year, and the effect it had on my mom and Daddy Lou's relationship was beginning to show. I would hear them arguing in their bedroom late at night, after my mom came home drunk from the bar where she'd met her lover. These arguments escalated into violence. In one particularly bad fight, my mom hit Daddy Lou over the head with a heavy antique stainless steel clothing iron, then stormed out of the house in a rage, leaving Daddy Lou on the floor, bleeding profusely.

I can't imagine the pain Daddy Lou must have been feeling at this point, both physical and emotional. It was bad enough to endure my mother's abuse, but to know she was also cheating on him—it brings me to the verge of tears, even today, when I think back on how much he must have been hurting. I loved Daddy Lou dearly, and my brothers too; it was for them that I'd moved back home in the first place. The trauma and anxiety of living with my mom again was too much, though. Seeing her beat up on Daddy Lou brought back my memories of watching her hit him when I'd been younger and of the beatings she had doled out to me and my brothers. It was too much for me to bear, and Cesar saw how I was suffering. We didn't live there long before we decided it was best to move back in with Joey and Mary.

Things had changed after Cesar and I had moved away. Joey and Mary were now living in a big one-story house with a lot of extra rooms that they rented out to families, turning the home into a kind of boardinghouse. Jenny lived in one of the rooms, and after we moved in, I grew even closer to her. She quickly became my best friend. I was fourteen going on fifteen, a full-blown young woman, and in Mary's eyes that meant I would need to earn my keep, even though Cesar paid rent for our room, like all the other boarder families did. One of the services included in the boarders' rent was laundry, so once a week Mary, Jenny, and I would spend a few hours at the local washateria taking care of everyone's sheets and clothes. The rest of the week, there were plenty of other chores to keep me busy, and while I didn't realize it at the time, I was trapped in my own home.

Mary was the authority figure in my life while we lived at the boardinghouse, at times almost like a mother. She battled her own array of inner demons, though they were different from the ones my mom struggled with. Joey was Mary's third husband, and her children from her first two marriages had rejected her: they didn't share a close bond or talk to each other often. One of her previous husbands had died, and though she had built a good life with Joey, he was a womanizer and an alcoholic, and I don't think she was very happy in their marriage. All this pain was, I think, a large part of why she could be so domineering around the house, shouldering the role of mother for everyone under her roof. A lot of her actions weren't particularly Christian either; Jenny told me Mary was a practitioner of bad magic and she paid a *brujo*, or witch doctor, thousands of dollars to help her put hexes on her enemies. She had no qualms about using manipulation to make financial gains, even if it harmed the people she loved. I could understand why her relationship with her children was complicated, but at first, she was generally nice to me, treating me like a daughter. Maybe, like Daddy Lou, she saw me as a stand-in for the children who were gone.

I started to look forward to our weekly trips to the washateria, and not just because they gave me a chance to get out of the house. There were three brothers from the neighborhood who also did their laundry there. All of them were married with families and worked the night shift, which was why we'd see them around the neighborhood taking care of chores during the day. Mary, Jenny, and I made it a habit to always do our laundry the same day as the brothers, and soon we were all friends. Talking with them helped the time to pass while we waited. They were good company—especially Eli. He was twenty-nine, fourteen years older than me. He was married, and I was with Cesar, but that didn't stop either of us from flirting with each other.

It was around this time that life with Cesar started to take a turn for the worse. He was drinking more and more, coming home from the bars belligerent and ready to fight. Even when he was sober, he wasn't emotionally available. It was as if all he could feel was rage and jealousy. Sometimes he'd come home with hickeys on his neck; I suspected he had a lover at the bar—possibly the bartender, though I didn't know for sure. On some weekends after Cesar left to go out, Mary and Joey took Jenny and me out to the dance clubs. I felt like a princess on those nights. Jenny and I did each other's makeup and hair and I'd often wear a new dress—Cesar did give me money for clothes. I always had a line of men waiting their turn to dance with me. Amid all the darkness I was living with, these nights out gave me a taste of the light. I learned all different kinds of dancing from my partners. One night, my partner and I even won first place in a salsa-dancing contest. We got a gift card and flowers. I still remember dancing, spinning, watching the neon lights, my face glowing. I felt like Cinderella.

***

But just as with Cinderella, once I was home again, the magic of those nights out dancing was replaced by the grim reality of my life. I felt like a prisoner, isolated and frustrated and still desperately searching for someone to love me in a normal, healthy way, which I knew Cesar could never do. I started an affair with Eli to fill that gap. Our affair was a passionate whirlwind, and it didn't take long for Cesar to find out. It's no wonder. Eli and I weren't exactly subtle; he only lived about three homes away and would sometimes drive by, honking his horn and blowing kisses.

One weekend, a noise woke me up in the middle of the night. I heard yelling outside but didn't realize what was going on until Cesar stormed in. He'd confronted Eli about our affair and had come into the bedroom in a fit of rage. He called me a whore, and I struck back, taunting him by saying he was less of a man than Eli was. In response, Cesar slapped me across my face, leaving me speechless.

Back when my mother had beaten me, I'd had no one to protect me; not even Daddy Lou could keep her from harming me, though he had tried. But now, Cesar had been drinking with Joey before the confrontation started, and even in his inebriated state, Joey saw that things had gone too far. He saw my swollen face and told Cesar to never hit me in front of him or under his roof. Cesar listened—for the night, at least. Soon, though, we fell into a pattern all too familiar to survivors of domestic abuse. Cesar would have a violent mood swing, lash out with abuse, then apologize profusely, promising that it would never happen again. After each incident, there'd be a honeymoon phase, a week or two of peace, but it never lasted.

I started having mood swings of my own, similar to the ones I'd witnessed in my own mother. I continued my affair with Eli, but even that wasn't enough anymore. I moved on to Eli's cousin; a chain of affairs followed. I would pull in men with the promise of love until they were hooked on me, then disappear once my physical needs had been met. Maybe I was just leaving them before they could leave me. Or maybe I was making them pay for what my abusers had done to me when I was a child. Whatever the reason, my promiscuity only made Cesar's jealousy and possessiveness worse.

I started working at a local cafeteria to escape him. It was a more complicated process than it should have been; I didn't have a social security card because my mom had never bothered to get one for me. In those days, though, you could get a job with a fake name and social security number, and that's what I did. Since I didn't drive, Cesar would drop me off and pick me up. I think he also wanted to keep an eye on me. He was jealous of my manager at the cafeteria, a kind and handsome blue-eyed man named James. His suspicions weren't entirely unfounded. I had a crush on James, and I think he felt the same about me, but we didn't act on our mutual attraction because he was married and committed to his young wife.

Things at home started to go from bad to worse. Cesar's drinking was out of control, and he was more violent than ever when he came home. In one of the worst incidents, he threatened to kill me and tried to stab me with a screwdriver. He managed to hit my left thumb, but I got away and locked myself in the car until he calmed down. I was terrified of what Cesar would do next.

First, he forced me to quit my job, but I still had Joey to protect me, and I could talk with Mary and Jenny. To further isolate me, we would have to move out, which was why Cesar agreed to move to Detroit with me when I suggested it. My uncle Bert lived there, and I thought he might be able to help me get my real social security card so I could get a job legally and free myself from Cesar.

Bert opened his home to us, but he wasn't around very often, and his work as a bartender kept him out late into the night. Cesar found a job working the graveyard shift at a tortilla factory, and I stayed home. The houses in Detroit were different from the ones I was used to in Dallas. They were big, old two- and three-story homes with neglected basements and attics inhabited by huge rats. While the setting was different, nothing had really changed. Cesar would still go out drinking and come home angry in the early morning hours, demanding sex and slapping me if I refused. My only solace was that he held off on beating me more severely out of fear my uncle would hear him and intervene. I knew it was only a matter of time before things got worse again. I started planning how I would make my escape.

There wasn't much I could do without a social security card, so I had Bert take me to the city's social security office. The only document I had was an old birth certificate I had taken from my mother a while back, and I wasn't sure if this would be enough to get the card. Thankfully, this was another moment when God's grace touched my life. The person who helped me at the office was a kindly older man. He looked at the birth certificate and told me that if Bert was willing to sign an affidavit in my support, he would issue the documentation. A few weeks later, I was the proud owner of a new social security card.

And this lifeline was arriving just in time. My life at home was constant violence. Once Cesar got comfortable with Bert's routines, he started beating me again when Bert wasn't home. Cesar also stopped taking no for an answer when he came home at night, forcing me to have sex with him whether I wanted to or not. I was so terrified of Cesar's beatings that I resorted to hiding in the attic with the rats, frozen in the fetal position, afraid to move in case it would draw their attention. Anxiety, shame, and fear were my only companions during these dark weeks. I had to get back to Dallas and the relative safety of Joey's protection. I cried and begged until Cesar finally relented. We moved back to Dallas just five months after we'd left, settling in again with Joey and Mary.

***

By this point, I knew Cesar was a ticking time bomb, but I don't think I realized how close he was to exploding. I tried not to think about it. I was just relieved to be back in the relative safety of Dallas and set about restoring my life to the way it had been before we'd gone to Detroit. I got my job back at the cafeteria, though I had to lie to Cesar to do it, telling him that James wasn't the manager there anymore, even though he was.

James was still happily married, so I turned my attentions to a cook at the cafeteria, a young man who was just as full of sexual energy as I was at the time. One night in late April 1984, I stayed with James after closing in the hope I could arrange to get a few days off for my lover and myself. Little did I know that Cesar had been out with one of his cousins. Drunk and angry, he'd come to the cafeteria to check up on me and had been watching me through the window of the main dining room while I talked to James. He was waiting at the door when I went to leave. I was baffled at first when he opened the door for me, but the second I saw the rage in his eyes, I was gripped by fear. He walked me into the dark parking lot, where he delivered the most vicious beating I'd ever experienced. It was so severe, I was knocked unconscious, waking up hours later in the ER with a pounding headache and my face sore and bloodied. I suffered a broken nose and lacerations to my lip and around my eye, and one of my teeth had been chipped when I'd fallen onto my face on the concrete.

Cesar and my cousin took me to the ER after I collapsed. I probably would have still gone home with Cesar that night, despite the brutality of his latest beating, if it hadn't been for one of my nurses. She was an older woman with snow-white hair, wearing a dress of the same spotless white, and her face glowed with serenity. When she saw that I was awake, she begged me to tell her who had beaten me. She held my hand and told me that Jesus loved me, and I felt safe with her in a way I hadn't in a long time. I confessed that my boyfriend was abusing me, and the nurse convinced me to press charges. Another nurse came in and had me sign an affidavit saying that he had been the perpetrator of the attack. Not long after, the white-haired nurse came back and showed me to the hallway, pointing toward where Cesar was being handcuffed by police officers. While they escorted him to the police car, she told me I should leave Cesar for good and that he would never hurt me again.

I spent the night in the ER. When I woke the next morning, a different nurse was attending me. I asked about the nice older woman who'd spoken to me the night before, but none of the daytime nurses seemed to know who I was talking about and couldn't think of anyone who worked there matching the description I gave. I never again saw that nurse who'd spoken to me of Jesus, and I am certain her presence in my hospital room that night was a divine intervention. She was a true angel, sent to free me from Cesar's control over my life and the pain he had inflicted on me.

Cesar was in jail for two weeks—the best two weeks I'd had for ages and the first time I felt truly safe. Once he was released, he was deported to Mexico, giving me some physical distance from him. That didn't stop him from calling me, though, which he did every day. He apologized endlessly for having injured me, promising he would make it up to me with a real wedding in Mexico. He told me he'd saved up money there and could truly take care of me, the way he'd always promised. Rationally, I knew these promises were a lie, but only a person who has been a victim of domestic violence can understand the way the abuse twists your thoughts. I wanted to believe Cesar really did care for me, that this time was different. Just like when I was a child, fantasy was more appealing than reality, and it was about to bring a whole new level of anguish into my life.

4

Abduction

Though she was nice to me when I was living in her house, Aunt Mary didn't have my best interests at heart. She could be a manipulative woman, and I watched her exploit her daughter, Jenny, whom she made do chores around the house to pay for her keep. At times, Jenny was forced to perform sexual favors for money so she could pay Mary the full room and board. Mary did the same with me, encouraging me to date men so I could bring home more money for her. I didn't realize how far Mary would go, however, or that she was in cahoots with Cesar. I was still innocent and naive in this regard and had no inkling of what Mary was capable of.

Mary's ruse was simple. She told me we were just going to take a quick trip across the border for Mother's Day to say hello to Cesar and his mom, Betty, whom he was living with now that he was back in Mexico. Mary said she would come pick me up after a few hours and we'd go back to Dallas.

We drove across the border from McAllen, Texas, to Reynosa, Mexico, where we met Cesar and his mother at a restaurant. When his mom went to the bathroom, Cesar grabbed my hand and dragged me outside, where I saw a black car with dark tinted windows waiting for us. He took a big pocketknife out of his pocket and shoved it against my ribs. "You're mine," he told me. "Don't try to run, or I'll kill you."

I thought about screaming, but there was no one around to hear. Instead, I broke free from Cesar's grip and ran straight across the plaza. Cesar caught me, subdued me, and pulled me into the black car. A few people looked at us, but no one stepped in to help. After driving several feet, the car took a sharp turn, and we picked his mom up at the corner. Then we were on our way back to their home, more than five hours' drive deeper into Mexico.

It was only later that I learned the truth: Cesar had paid Mary $500 to bring me into Mexico. Not only that, but Mary had both my birth certificate and my social security card. I had no money of my own and no identification proving I was a US citizen. Even if I managed to slip away from Cesar, I'd have nowhere to go. I was trapped in a foreign country, against my will, with my abuser—the start of a new horrific episode in the nightmare that had become my life.

Though I was just sixteen years old and legally still a child, I knew one thing for certain: nobody was looking for me.

***

Living in Mexico was a waking nightmare, one I couldn't escape from. Cesar and I shared a studio apartment behind the home where his mom lived with her second husband. This small space became my prison. There were iron bars on the windows and a handmade steel lock on the outside of the door to keep me from escaping. I was only allowed to eat or bathe when Cesar was around, usually late in the evening. Betty had the keys, and though she followed Cesar's instructions, I truly believed she felt guilty about helping her son hold me captive.

She took me to a restaurant once or twice a week on the days we went grocery shopping at the local *mercado*, a warehouse where different merchants sell produce, meat, clothing, and other things. She sometimes bought me small gifts like barrettes. She also confided in me, confirming what Cesar had said about his biological father beating both her and Cesar with sticks and belts, and telling me that there was nothing she could do to stop Cesar. Betty would also at times unlock my room to allow me some fresh air and time to watch the television. As a fellow victim of domestic and emotional abuse, I couldn't help but sympathize with her.

I knew Betty felt bad about how Cesar treated me, but in many ways, she was as dominated by him as I was. I could see she was racked with guilt over the abuse Cesar had witnessed and experienced as a child, and that guilt led her to forgive his behavior: she saw it as her fault, not his, since she'd failed to protect him when he was young. If it were another man abusing me, perhaps she would have spoken up, but she couldn't stand up to her own son, not when she had gotten him into the abusive situation that had started this cycle in the first place. I think Betty was also afraid of Cesar and the violence he was capable of. It was this combination of guilt and fear that kept her from speaking up on my behalf during the weeks of my captivity. The only way she would have gone against Cesar's wishes was if she truly believed she was doing so to protect him.

She said that she hadn't been a part of the plot to kidnap

me, that Cesar hadn't even told her his plans before they went to the border to pick me up. Like me, his mom had been deceived and was helpless to stop my abduction once the wheels were set in motion. My talks and shopping trips with Cesar's mom were a lifeline of sanity through my otherwise dark and traumatizing captivity. She helped me survive.

The only other times I was allowed out of our apartment were when Cesar took me out to dinner or to a party on the weekends—that is, if he wasn't at the bar. The nights he went drinking continued to be the worst. He would arrive home in the early mornings, aggressively demanding sex and raping me if I resisted. Even when he was sober, he controlled my every move. I couldn't even go to the bathroom without his permission. Doing so was to risk awakening his demons.

Sometimes he would take me to dance parties and other family gatherings. I enjoyed the chance to dress up and feel beautiful, but with that, too often, came the attention of young men. There would always be a few vying for my attention. Maybe they could see my pain and wanted to rescue me— which would be ironic, if that were the case, because they only ever made things worse. I could never tell what would provoke one of Cesar's jealous outbursts and spent most of these gatherings in silent terror, paralyzed by the fear that I would make the wrong move. What Cesar was really afraid of, I think, was that I would find a way to run and get back home. He was so insecure, so desperate to keep me, that he destroyed me inside.

Cesar did stay true to his promise to marry me, but even this was part of a larger plot. He and Mary had planned the whole thing out. They figured that if Cesar were married to me—a US citizen—it would allow him to get an American green card and legally return to the United States. Betty did her best to make my wedding day as tolerable as possible, even taking me to get my hair done at a salon. The hairdresser kept asking me, "Why are you so sad? You are getting married!" How could I tell her I was being forced to marry a monster? I knew I'd be killed if I did.

The ceremony itself wasn't exactly a fairy tale either. It was a small gathering paid for by Cesar's mom and stepdad, officiated by the magistrate they'd bribed for the license. There was a dinner with his friends and family and dancing afterward to celebrate. Cesar drank too much and started to get jealous of the male guests, which was ridiculous; I didn't even know anyone except Cesar and his family. One man simply asked Cesar how long we'd known each other, a benign question but enough to activate the jealous monster in him, and they ended up in a fight. By the end of the night, Cesar had forced himself on me. I was too scared to refuse. I was already emotionally numb, but this was the last straw, and I broke down completely.

Getting married should be a joyous occasion, and I'd once dreamed of how that perfect day would go. But in reality, it was anything but. I was totally cut off from everything I'd known; I missed my family and my old life. As the weeks passed, the stress and anxiety were so severe I had outbreaks of hives and welts all over my body that I couldn't stop scratching. I also had panic attacks on a regular basis; my identity, my sense of self, had been completely overwhelmed. I became very much like my mother: bitter and resentful, prone to intense anger. Living under constant terror and emotional strain was tearing me apart. Once again, Little Nikki emerged. She felt so lost, so alone, and so sad, and her only desire was to please so she could receive an ounce of love and approval. I remember letting Little Nikki speak for me in a soft voice so that perhaps the pain, both emotional and physical, could just melt away.

Eventually, my hives became so severe that Cesar's mom

took me to a doctor. Maybe the doctor sensed how distraught I was. Or maybe she felt something was off with Cesar's mom, because after noticing my bloody scratches, she asked Betty who'd done that to me, and Betty wouldn't answer. Whatever the reason, the doctor wouldn't allow her to come into the exam room with us.

Once we were alone, I started sobbing.

"Who is the woman that brought you here?" she asked.

"Cesar's mom," I told her, shaking as I cried even harder.

After more prompting, I told her everything: about being tricked into coming to Mexico and the abduction that followed, how Cesar was abusing me and keeping me trapped and isolated. The doctor told me there was a human rights law in Mexico. She could look into it, she said, and find a way to get me out of this horrible situation.

She diagnosed me with urticaria, a skin condition caused by acute emotional distress, and prescribed me medicine for it, as well as Tofranil for my anxiety, but she knew that was just a temporary fix. It could help with the symptoms, maybe, but no medication would extract me from this nightmare I was living. She scheduled a follow-up visit so we could talk more about the human rights program she'd mentioned, but even that didn't seem like it would be of much help to me. I didn't know anyone in Mexico other than Cesar and his mom, and without any form of identification, I couldn't get back into the United States. Even if I escaped from Cesar, I had nowhere else to go.

It was all so hopeless.

Afterward, she called Betty into the exam room while I went out to the waiting room. I was terrified the entire time Betty was in there with her. I didn't want Betty to tell Cesar what I'd told the doctor.

I don't know exactly what the doctor said to Betty, but Betty emerged looking angry and concerned. She peppered me with questions about what I'd said to the doctor and finally told me she had to get me out of the country before Cesar found out what I'd done and killed me.

This doctor was one of my angels in Mexico. So was Betty. It's incredible the ways that people can have a profound impact on your life even if they're in it for only a short time.

***

About a week later, Betty came into my room while Cesar was at work and told me to get dressed. She said we were going to go shopping and grab a bite to eat. I knew right away something strange was going on. It wasn't our usual market day, and Cesar was normally quite strict about me staying at home on days he hadn't approved of my helping with errands. I got dressed and followed her to a waiting taxi. It was only once we were on the road that she told me what was really going on. She said she was afraid her son was going to kill me, and she could no longer allow Cesar to beat me and keep me as his prisoner.

Betty had called Mary and asked her to bring my birth certificate and social security card and meet us at the border. She said she'd told Cesar we were just meeting Mary to retrieve some of my things, which were all still back in the United States. After all, I hadn't planned to be in Mexico for more than a few hours when I'd set out with Mary on the trip that had begun this nightmare. The real reason for our trip, though, was that Betty wanted to help me escape. Once I had proof of my identity, I would be able to get back across the border and into Texas, where Cesar couldn't legally follow me.

We made the five-hour bus ride to the border crossing in Laredo, Texas. When we arrived, though, Mary wasn't there. It turned out that Cesar had called Mary, and she'd told him what Betty and I were really doing at the border. Once he'd found out I planned to escape, Cesar had told Mary not to bring my documents, knowing that without those, I had no hope of returning to my home country. Betty called Mary from the border, begging her to come and help me, but she refused.

I didn't know what to do. I couldn't go back to Cesar. I had been afraid of him before, but now I was absolutely terrified, thinking of what he might do to me now that he knew I had tried to escape. Eventually, Betty suggested we go into the immigration office and talk to the officers on duty to see if there was anything they could do to help. I was an American citizen, after all, even if I didn't have the documents on hand to prove it. Cesar's mom did at least have the wedding certificate from my marriage to Cesar, proof that she was my mother-in-law, but this, we would soon learn, was not nearly enough to earn me passage back into the United States.

It's hard to explain the muddle of emotions you live with every moment of every day as a victim of domestic violence. The environment of constant fear made it hard to think and react rationally in response to the things around me. Even when he was hours away, Cesar's shadow was always darkening my thoughts, and I was always on the defensive, trying to shield myself against them.

The immigration officials didn't believe me right away when I told them I was being held in Mexico against my will. I think they wanted to believe a story like mine couldn't be possible. More than anything, I think they were baffled by how an American citizen had ended up in the situation I was in. The fact that I spoke fluent English seemed to confuse them rather than confirm my story. It was inconceivable to them that a sixteen-year-old girl from Texas could be held captive for nearly two months in Mexico without anyone looking for her or raising an alarm over her disappearance. I imagine they'd never seen a situation like mine, but they likely had caught countless young women trying to talk their way into the US under false pretenses. It was much easier for them to believe I was making up stories than to wrap their heads around the truth.

I'm sure my appearance didn't help either. I still had scabs from the urticaria and hadn't showered in I don't know how many days, so my hair was stringy and dirty. Betty had tried to get me to take a shower before we'd left, but I had been angry and refused to do so. I'd told her that *they* were the ones who'd made me dirty, that her son had forced her to keep me locked up and I didn't care how I looked.

The officers separated me from Betty and took me into an interrogation room inside the immigration building. The stress of the situation activated my usual survival instinct: to shut down and detach myself emotionally. Little Nikki was always there, watching, observant of every detail. In an effort to protect this part of myself, I rebelled in anger against the officers. Their aggression was too much like my mom's, too much like Cesar's, too much like all the people in my life who had tried to control me, and Little Nikki was reliving the trauma. I began to shut down and retreat into my own world to protect her. From the way they were speaking to me, it seemed like they were more interested in punishing me for crimes I hadn't committed than they were in helping me. This made me even more combative in my responses to their questions, which in turn seemed to convince them even more strongly that I was lying. I refused to let them intimidate me, though.

The officers interrogated me for several hours. At first, they asked me about my parents. I told them I didn't have any parents, angrily shouting, "I don't have a mother! I wasn't born from anyone!" This felt true to me at the time; I'd never known my biological father, and the last time I'd spoken to my mother, she'd told me I was dead to her. Certainly, though, this response didn't help them view me as a cooperative victim. My fear of Cesar also made it difficult for me to adequately convey my situation to the immigration officers: I was terrified of what he would do to me if he found out I'd accused him of abducting me, especially if I wasn't able to get back to the United States. Already I knew he would be angry with me for leaving; I feared for my life if he learned that I'd tried to have him arrested on top of that. When they asked me how I'd ended up in Mexico, I gave them a brief account of being taken and held against my will and explained where I had been living, but the officers questioning me weren't convinced, and I couldn't produce any evidence to support my claims. All we had was the Mexican marriage certificate, but the officers knew anyone could get a marriage certificate in Mexico if they bribed the right officials. They doubted its authenticity. Even if it was real, all it proved was that I was Cesar's wife. It could do nothing to show I was a United States citizen.

Over the course of the day, I was questioned by a number of different officers, who kept demanding I tell them the truth. I think they assumed I was either a drug smuggler or a sex worker, asking me over and over who my contacts were in Mexico and what my pimp's name was.

When it got late enough, I was shown into a room with a little cot, where I could sleep and rest while I waited for the next round of interrogation. I might have ended up in an actual jail cell or been left to fend for myself alone in Mexico, but after hours of questioning, I again received a moment of God's grace, this time in the form of a kind immigration officer. He had a daughter of his own, I learned as we talked, and it pained him to see a young girl in my situation. He said that he wanted to help me, but he needed my help to figure out how he could do that. The other officers had been aggressive in their questioning. That was how they'd been trained, I've realized, and they thought they were just doing their jobs. But this kind officer spoke to me with sympathy, not suspicion. His compassion was like a little sign from God, telling me this was a person who wouldn't hurt me, and that made me feel safe enough to drop the angry, defensive shield I'd maintained during the earlier hours of questioning. Little Nikki was so exhausted and vulnerable at this point, and I could no longer hold back her river of tears.

My tough exterior crumbled as I broke down and told the officer everything that had happened to me. I told him about Mary taking me to the border on false pretenses and being abducted at knifepoint from the restaurant parking lot. I explained where I was living, that I was being abused and kept there against my will, and that I feared for my life if I was made to go back. The officer listened with the attentive ear of a protective father, and, unlike the others, when I finished talking, I could see that he believed me.

The officer asked me for Mary's phone number, and I gave them the landline for the house in Dallas. He told her that what she'd done was criminal and that she could and would be prosecuted as an abductor if she didn't arrive at the border with my birth certificate and social security card within twenty-four hours. Mary was obviously afraid of having legal action brought against her. She tried to cover up her role in the sinister plot she'd hatched with Cesar, blaming him for orchestrating the entire thing, but the officer was unmoved by her lies.

Based on what I'd told him of Mary's actions, the officer told me I could file charges against her if I wanted to, but I declined to sign the accusation. I was afraid of Mary too, in a different way. She wasn't violent and abusive like Cesar was, but I had seen the black candles she kept in her room and how she used them for her bad magic and hexes. After everything I had endured already in my life, having Mary put a hex on me was the last thing I needed. Besides, I knew that—like most people with evil in their hearts—Mary was ultimately a coward when it came to justice. Now that her dark dealings with Cesar had been brought into the light, she'd risk facing real punishment if she hurt me again. That wasn't a risk she would take, I knew, especially when the fatherly immigration officer told me he'd had a nice long chat with Mary. He had her number and information now. If she hurt me or helped Cesar do so again, he could turn the information I'd given him over to higher authorities and pursue charges even without a formal accusation from me.

The drive from Dallas to Laredo is long, eight hours at least, but the threat of criminal charges lit a fire under Mary. She arrived at the border with the documents proving my US citizenship well before the officer's twenty-four-hour deadline. When she did, her demeanor was completely transformed from that of the Mary I'd always known. She was on her best behavior, putting on a show of being concerned about my well-being and apologizing profusely for what Cesar had done to me. I knew it was fake, although I do think there was a part of Mary that wanted me to escape. Mary had never been above doing unsavory things, but plotting a kidnapping so her nephew could get a green card was extreme even by her standards. I think she felt guilty and regretted her role in my abduction, and that guilt was as responsible for her behavioral shift as her fear of legal consequences was.

Before we left the immigration center, the kindly officer warned Mary again that he was keeping my file open, and both she and Cesar would be held accountable for my well-being. Thanks to his intervention, I was finally going back home to Dallas and would be safe from Cesar.

Or so I thought.

5

Aftershocks

By this point, it was July 1984. I went back to the old routines of my life in Dallas before the abduction. I moved back into Mary and Joey's house, taking on my share of the cleaning and other chores. Mary was still a completely different person around me; she seemed on edge and cautious, as though at any moment I might change my mind and decide to have her arrested after all.

My mom and Daddy Lou didn't live too far away from Mary's. Once I got back from Mexico, my mom was in my life again. My youngest brother, Ronald, had been born in September 1983, and at one point, I left Mary's for a week or so to go stay at my mom and Daddy Lou's home. I had the opportunity to parent Ronald, who was only about nine months old and a wonderful baby.

Mary and my mom didn't get along at all, and Mary would use all she knew of Daddy Lou and his family—and the wife he'd had before my mom—to fuel her arguments. Once, things escalated to a point where Mary pulled a knife on my mom. It was just a small blade, one of those little folding pocket-knives, but she still cut my mom's arm and face with it. I think my mom was hesitant to come around to Mary and Joey's place because of these incidents, but I saw her often enough that I could begin to form a new relationship with her. This was when I started being able to forgive her. For a long time, I had been bitter toward my mother because of the pain and abuse she had subjected me to. The turning point came once I started to see her as a victim too, and someone who deserved my compassion.

I also saw my mom's objections to Cesar differently, in light of what had happened. When she'd initially refused to sign the marriage certificate, I had thought she'd just been trying to be mean and keep me from having the happiness I deserved. Now that I'd seen Cesar's true colors, I realized that, in her own way, my mom had been trying to protect me. Since my mom hadn't allowed us to get married in the United States, I was now free from Cesar, and he couldn't use me to legally enter the country. I'd learned during my time at the immigration office in Laredo that the marriage certificate from Mexico wasn't valid. As I'd told them, I'd never been asked to show my birth certificate when Cesar had gotten the marriage license. He had bribed an official to obtain the license without providing the necessary paperwork, and it turned out that, just like in the United States, a minor needed a guardian's permission to be married, and obviously my mom hadn't granted that permission.

My relationship with Cesar was certainly not one you could define with any traditional terms, but I had thought of him as my husband. We had lived like a married couple even before he'd abducted me in Mexico, and after we'd had the wedding ceremony there, I'd assumed it had been legal and official. Finding out that license had been a sham was initially a shock but ultimately a relief. If we'd never really been married, Cesar and I had no legal ties to each other. It was one less thing he could use to try and force his way back into my life.

I wasn't naive enough to think this would keep Cesar from trying to take me back, though. I knew that he was still in communication with Mary and was sure she'd told him that I was staying with her. Whenever the phone rang at the house, I'd stand out of sight in the hallway leading to the living room and listen in on Mary's side of the conversation. It was only a matter of time, I figured, before Cesar and Mary concocted a new plan to smuggle him back into the United States. I wanted to be ready when that happened. He had surprised me the first time, exploiting my innocence and trusting nature. I was determined not to make that mistake again.

My hypervigilance wasn't the only lingering effect of my captivity. The hives and rashes I'd had in Mexico started to fade, but I've continued to have psychosomatic symptoms in times of emotional stress throughout my life. Often this takes the form of stomachaches or migraines. Over time, I've learned to take these as signs that I'm feeling emotionally overwhelmed and need to undertake some self-care, but at sixteen, I hadn't yet developed that level of insight into my inner psyche. I was still very much emotionally underdeveloped, my interior growth having been stunted by the abuse I'd been subjected to since I was a small child. I was starting to learn how to stand up for myself and to gain my own sense of identity, but that was a healing process that would take years, and I was only at the beginning of it.

***

Once I had settled back into life in Dallas, I started to feel out the edges of this newfound freedom. I knew better than to think Cesar was out of my life forever, no matter how much I hoped and wished that could be the case. Over time, though, I was able to stop worrying so much about what Cesar would think and start living my life again. Despite everything I'd already experienced, I was still just a teenage girl. Most girls my age were enjoying their first courtships, feeling the first stirrings of puppy love with their high school sweethearts and giggling about it with their friends. I had missed out on having these kinds of experiences, so it felt like something of a novelty to do things that would be normal for other teenagers, like going to a party or Spanish dance hall. It's probably why I didn't even think about going back to school. I felt older than my years, but I also wanted to catch up on all the fun things that I had missed. I was truly free to do what I wanted, when I wanted, for the first time, and I was cherishing it. I didn't want mundane things like homework holding me back.

I didn't have many friends in the area, so when I went out, it was usually with Jenny, Mary, and Joey. This was during the phase when Mary's guilt was still fresh and she was being especially friendly and kind toward me. Jenny was newly single, just like me; her husband had revealed himself to be an alcoholic, and their marriage had failed after a little over a year. When we all went out together, though, it didn't seem to matter that Joey and Mary's relationship was unhappy or that Mary had betrayed my trust and sold me out to Cesar. It was a chance to forget about all that for a little while. Despite all the drama and conflict in our past, we usually ended up having fun, something I had been sorely lacking for far too long.

I was at one of those dance halls when I met Charles that July. He was handsome, about five feet, six inches, with black hair and a beard and mustache. It was more than his looks, though; I was drawn to who he was as a person. Both Jenny and I had enjoyed flirting with the boys at the clubs, reveling in their attention, but I knew Charles was different from the rest as soon as I met him. I could just tell he was a good man. Charles had also recently gotten out of a bad relationship, having broken up with his live-in girlfriend not long before we met. He was about ten years older than me, with an almost fatherly energy that I craved. The age difference didn't matter when we talked. He was a true adult with a good job as a supervisor at a local steel company, which I was drawn to as well. I'd had enough of the instability of my younger years.

I knew it would be impossible to keep our relationship a secret from Mary since I lived with her. Luckily, I also knew she was greedy. I gave her money and begged her not to tell Cesar about Charles, and she agreed that she wouldn't as long as I kept up with the cooking and chores I did to pay for my room and board. For the first few weeks, it seemed as though she'd kept her promise—she didn't even comment when Charles picked me up from the house for a date. Our courtship was fast and intense but refreshingly normal in comparison to my relationship with Cesar. We'd go out to dinner, catch a movie, or sometimes just hang out and talk while we walked around the mall.

The more I learned about Charles, the more I loved him. He was incredibly romantic, bringing flowers when he picked me up for dates and writing me cute cards and love letters to express his affection. Once, he took me out to a nice Mexican restaurant and gave me a beautiful gold promise ring. I'd never felt so loved as I did that night. It was like I was living in a fairy tale. It didn't really matter what we did; as long as I was with Charles, I felt safe and happy.

At least, I felt as safe as I could with the dark cloud of Cesar's possible return hovering over me. I knew, deep down, that my arrangement with Mary had only delayed the inevitable. Cesar would eventually learn about Charles, and I had no doubt Mary would be the one to tell him. I was hypervigilant when I was at the house, always listening for the ring of the phone and creeping down to the hallway to where I could eavesdrop on the conversation. I knew Mary was plotting to get Cesar back into the United States, but it was a complicated process. I would hear them arguing about finding someone who could smuggle him in. For the moment, he was still stuck in Mexico, but there was no telling how long that would last.

Charles knew all about my history with Cesar. I'd described the violence and abduction to him, showing him the scar on my thumb where Cesar had stabbed me with a screwdriver, and told him that I would fear for my life if Cesar managed to get back into the United States. When we were out on dates, I was worried that Mary had followed us, and I insisted that Charles take different routes each time he picked me up. He did everything he could to cheer me up when we were out, wiping away my tears and promising to protect me, but I could tell he wanted to do even more. I think growing up with four sisters made Charles especially sympathetic to my past and gave him an even stronger desire to protect me from further violence. He thought we should move in with Cristy, his eldest sister, who lived in a town called Richardson that was a few miles north of Dallas—close enough that we wouldn't have to uproot our lives but far enough, he hoped, that Cesar wouldn't be able to find me. I was relieved and instantly agreed. By the time September 1984 came around, we started preparing for the move.

But Mary had been so nice and accommodating since my return that I'd let my guard down. One day she casually asked me about my plans with Charles, and I told her about our upcoming move. It wasn't long after that I heard the old rotary phone ring. I snuck down to hide in the hallway, brimming with anxiety as Mary told Cesar he should hurry up and get the smugglers to bring him back to the United States now because I was dating another man and Cesar was about to lose me.

Over the next couple of days, I listened intently to their conversations, taking note of every detail. Then the call I'd been dreading finally came: Cesar had arrived at the border. By the next day, he'd be back in the United States. I knew I had to act quickly. I went to Jenny and asked her if she could keep Mary distracted while I made my escape. Unlike Mary, Jenny had always truly been on my side, and I knew she would help me get to safety however she could. Once she agreed, I quickly called Charles at the steel company, telling him what I'd heard and that I was on my way to meet him. I was frantic by the time I arrived. Charles wiped away my tears and told me to wait in his car while he went to talk to his boss. I couldn't stop thinking about Cesar's jealous rages the entire time I waited; I was afraid he would kill us both if he found us. But then Charles returned, and we were on the road, headed toward safety.

The apartment in Richardson where Cristy lived with her husband and baby wasn't large, but they were able to convert their nursery room into a place for Charles and me to stay. I knew from talking to Charles that he came from a very tight-knit family, and I could sense that closeness as soon as we stepped into Cristy's home. She was friendly and welcoming, making me feel accepted, and I could tell she and Charles respected each other in a way I'd never seen between family members. For the first time in many years, I felt at peace.

Over the next couple of weeks, I set about building my new life in Richardson. One thing I knew I needed was a source of income. As much as I appreciated Charles and his family taking care of me, I didn't want to rely on him the way I'd relied on Cesar. I talked to James, my old manager, about getting my job back at the cafeteria in Dallas. He couldn't rehire me, but he put in a good word with the manager of the Richardson location—which, to be honest, was a better option, anyway. It was closer to where I was living now, for one thing. Besides, Cesar knew I'd worked at that cafeteria; his violent confrontation with me in the parking lot was the main reason James couldn't hire me back. I felt like there was less of a chance Cesar would find me if I worked at a different location. I was hired as a food server, as was one of Charles's other sisters, Minnie, shortly after I started the job.

Unfortunately, I had underestimated the lengths to which Cesar would go in his obsession to track me down. About a month after he returned to the United States, he started hounding my former coworkers about whether they'd seen me and where he could find me. One of the people Cesar questioned was a man who'd come on to me repeatedly when we worked together. He was still bitter over the way I'd refused his sexual advances and now told Cesar that I'd been rehired and worked at the cafeteria in Richardson.

Cesar started stalking me, camping out near the restaurant so he could watch me come and go, learning my schedule. At the end of my shift one night, Cesar ambushed Charles and me outside the restaurant. We had just gotten to Charles's car, but I was too stunned by the sight of Cesar to get myself inside. I started screaming, paralyzed by the terror gripping every corner of my soul, certain that I was going to die. If I had been alone, Cesar may very well have murdered me that night or abducted me again. I shudder to think what kind of captivity he would have subjected me to, how much tighter he would have controlled my every move now that I'd escaped from him once before.

Thankfully, I wasn't alone. Charles made me get in the car and told me to lock the doors. Once I was safe, he told Cesar to leave me alone. Cesar threatened him, shouting that I was a bigamist for dating Charles and insisting we were still legally married in Mexico. Charles tried to defuse the situation, telling Cesar it should be my choice and suggesting he give me a couple of days to think it over. But Cesar was adamant. He wasn't going to leave unless I came with him.

Fortunately for me, Minnie was also working that night. She saw the confrontation in the parking lot as she was leaving the cafeteria and went back inside to call the police. As soon as the police car arrived, Cesar sprinted back to his old truck and sped off into the night, well aware that if he were arrested it would likely get him deported back to Mexico. In my eyes, he was a coward in the face of justice.

I was in no state of mind to talk to the police. Charles talked to them on my behalf, telling them he would personally bring me in to file a protective order if Cesar tried to cause any more trouble. All I wanted was to have Cesar out of my life. Just hearing his name triggered memories, forcing me to relive the trauma. Cesar's wounds had cut so deeply into my soul that the only way to spare myself the pain was to avoid him entirely. It wasn't until after Cesar left that I found out the extent of the danger we'd been in. Charles admitted to me that during the confrontation, he'd seen that Cesar had been armed with a large pocketknife. He'd willingly risked violence, maybe even death, to protect me. Charles was truly my guardian angel.

Even with Charles by my side, however, I still couldn't feel completely safe. If Cesar knew where I worked, what would stop him from finding out where I was living? I was constantly afraid that he would attack me or Charles again, and that next time, there might not be anyone around to help. I quit my job at the cafeteria—it would be too easy to find me there, and that made it too much of a risk—and began working at Dallas Dusters, cleaning houses. I was making $500 a week with tips. That was a lot back in 1984, especially for a young girl with no education. I was on cloud nine. I had a lot of ambition and wanted to buy a car and even a home. Also, the holidays were just around the corner, and earning money brought me joy and made me feel pretty independent. I felt like I was finally coming into my own.

Around that same time, I sent a message to Mary through a mutual friend, telling her I would press domestic abuse charges against Cesar if he came near me again. One thing I could count on from Mary was that she would always look out for her own self-interests. She knew that, at any time, I could reach out to the immigration officer who still had a file open on her and put her in the same legal trouble Cesar would be in if I filed charges. My hope was that she would talk him into keeping away from me to stay in my good graces. Whether through Mary's influence or out of his own fear of being deported, Cesar backed off. After a few weeks passed with no more incidents, I started to let myself hope that I could have a normal life with Charles.

The next few months were some of the happiest I'd had in a long time. Living with Cristy was therapeutic. She was kind and empathetic, just like her brother, and she quickly became my closest friend. In the same way, being around Charles's siblings was my first experience being a part of a healthy, functional family. His mom and dad were loving parents. Though they were living in Mexico, they maintained close bonds with all their kids. And they had a lot of them: Charles had six siblings, four sisters and two brothers. Charles was the oldest, followed by Cristy, who was three years younger and the only one who was married with a family. For the rest of them, Charles happily filled the role of a good big brother, especially now that his younger sisters were old enough to date.

I felt like I had finally found a place where I could be safe and loved for who I was. After church on Sunday afternoons, Charles's sisters taught me how to do basic chores like ironing and sewing. Best of all, they taught me how to cook real Mexican food; all I'd known how to cook before was basic things my brothers liked to eat, like hot dogs and boxed mac and cheese. I also didn't know how to drive, so Charles offered to teach me that too, which meant I could get my driver's license one day, another stark contrast to my life with Cesar. Cesar had done everything he could to keep me trapped and dependent on him; Charles wanted me to have the skills and freedom I needed to be happy and self-sufficient.

6

Cracks in the Concrete

Our relationship, like the others in my life, had been a whirl-wind, so perhaps I shouldn't have been surprised that in November 1984, after I'd had a few days of nausea, Charles took me to the doctor for a checkup, and we learned I was pregnant.

I felt so many mixed emotions after learning I was carrying a child. I knew I had a lot of love to give, but I was also afraid. I didn't want to repeat the pattern, to become the same kind of angry, unloving mother my mom had been. I'd built so many protective mental walls. Would I be able to tear those down and share myself with my child, to form the close bonds healthy families seemed to forge so easily? Little Nikki resurfaced during this time; I would often feel a tingling in my belly that signaled her coming, along with my growing anxiety and fear. Little Nikki was overwhelmed and sad, feeling that she would be incapable of caring for the new baby. But it set my mind at ease to know Charles would be there to raise the child with me. He was very observant of my emotions and would just let Little Nikki hold him and sob. I told him how afraid I was, and he always reassured me, calling me his *muñequita*, little doll, and saying he would protect me. Little Nikki was calmed by this. She always yearned for her daddy, forever trying to find someone to fill that role. In January of the next year, we went out to a restaurant to celebrate, and he proposed to me, surrounded by his sisters and brothers. The ring was gorgeous, but it was the love I felt in that room that made the moment so memorable for me.

Of course, there were a few hurdles we had to clear before we could be married. First, we went together to the Mexican Consulate in Dallas and confirmed that my marriage to Cesar hadn't been recorded in Texas as a legal marriage. However, I was still a minor. The only way I could get married was if my mom was willing to sign the license. We had been on better terms since my return from Mexico, but I was still afraid to ask for her signature, haunted by the memory of the unused wedding dress and how unhappy I'd been.

It was Charles who ended up asking her about the wedding. He told my mom that I was pregnant, and that the stability of a marriage would be good for both me and the baby. I imagine it was the thought of having a grandchild that swayed my mom into agreeing. She trusted Charles too, I think, and I couldn't help but wonder if she felt guilty for how she'd handled things with Cesar. She hadn't kept me from seeing him, but in cutting me off, she'd driven a wedge between me and the rest of my family that made it easier for him to isolate me and exert even more influence over my life. Now she had a chance to do things over, knowing Charles was a good man who would take care of me and really wanted me to be happy.

Whatever her reasoning, my mom was there with us when we went to the courthouse in February 1985 to get married. With the baby on the way, we'd decided it was best to have a simple civil ceremony. Cristy and my mom served as witnesses. Afterward, we went out to eat to celebrate, and Charles told me he was going to join his family's Adventist church so that we could plan a real ceremony down the line. Years before, when I'd planned to marry Cesar, I had never gotten the fairytale wedding I'd dreamed of. Now I'd found my true Prince Charming, and I had another chance to live that dream.

Charles had resisted becoming a member of the church until now because he was not ready to settle down. He enjoyed drinking and going to the dance halls, both of which were prohibited by the church's strict doctrine. His father was a recovering alcoholic and had been verbally and emotionally abusive to his mother during his drinking days. He had joined the church when Charles was eighteen, though, and had gotten sober. His parents feared that Charles was heading in that same direction, so they'd been pressuring him to join as well.

I was so happy Charles was going to stop drinking after watching Daddy Lou's struggles with alcohol, but I didn't stop to think about what joining the church would mean for the both of us. I knew I'd have to join too, but I truly didn't understand all of what being a member entailed.

We knew we'd need more space once the baby arrived, so we started looking for a place to rent and found a beautiful two-story, five-bedroom brick home with room enough for me, Charles, our baby, Cristy, her husband, and their baby, along with two of Charles's other siblings, Minnie and Emiliano. When I called the landlord, he asked for a long list of qualifications, most of which I couldn't meet. But the house was perfect, and I didn't want to give up that easily. I told the landlord my story and how much it would mean to us to live in this home. God's grace again touched my life, and my words won him over. Even in my most difficult moments, I was never alone in my journey. God's angels were always there, pulling me through. Now they'd helped my deepest wish come true. This was exactly the kind of home I'd hoped to build when I'd left with Cesar all those years ago.

***

In June 1985, after an arduous sixteen-hour labor, I gave birth to my first son, John Charles. He was a small baby, only six and a half pounds, so precious and fragile it was almost hard to believe he could bring me so much joy. I was in awe of this little miracle God had given me. No feeling could compare to the happiness I felt holding my firstborn in my arms. My sisters-in-law instantly fell in love with their little nephew, and I had a lot of help taking care of him those first few months. Around this time, our lease expired, and Charles and I moved to an apartment, while Cristy and her husband bought their first home, about seven miles away from us. It was wonderful to be close, as Cristy was an excellent mother herself and helped me out frequently. I so wanted John to experience a loving family and was happy to be able to give him that.

My relationship with Charles was the first healthy romantic relationship I'd had in my life, but I hadn't begun the work of exorcising the angry demons I carried, and I struggled regularly with anxiety, jealousy, and anger. I buried that rage under the work of being a new mom, throwing myself into my marriage and my family rather than dealing with the emotions. Inevitably, though, they bubbled to the surface.

The main source of conflict in our marriage was Charles's

church. This Adventist church had very strict rules for members, especially women. Once you got married, you were supposed to submit to your husband. Attending dances and parties was forbidden, and women weren't supposed to wear makeup or jewelry. My sisters-in-law didn't have a problem with this; they were used to the strict rules. But I wasn't mentally prepared to make that shift. I wanted to have fun and go out with Charles like we used to before we were married, but he said we couldn't. The church wouldn't allow it. This new Charles was not the same man I'd fallen in love with—the one who liked to go out and dance and have fun, the one who saw women as equals, not chattel. The rules the church wanted its members to live by had turned him into a judgmental, controlling misogynist.

I began to rebel, buying clothes, jewelry, and makeup and wearing it to services. I could feel the disapproval from Charles and his sisters, which really stung. I didn't understand: I hadn't changed; they had. I truly didn't think I was doing anything wrong. I was still a teenager, after all, a seventeen-year-old with a baby who was just beginning to crawl, and on top of that, I worked. I was feeling overwhelmed. If I wanted to pamper myself a little bit, where was the harm in that?

I'd also begun to listen more closely to what the pastor said in his sermons, and I didn't like what I heard. He twisted scripture and said the true essence of beauty is in dressing modestly, but that women of "this day" tended to prefer vanity with elaborate hairstyles like perms. He said that things like engraved jewelry were a waste of money. He claimed you should give more of yourself by performing good deeds, and also encouraged women to work so they could turn over their own tithings in addition to what their husbands contributed.

While the pastor was continually quoting 1 Peter 3:3-4, I

did not agree with how he spoke about women in particular, all while male Church leaders had fallen into sin. In my simple understanding, I questioned his definition of the marriage covenant. Was it a lie unless it accommodated this pastor's view of women?

For example, while the male leaders' views of marriage were plain from a legal context, how could it also include the demands of willful slavery—as in, the true submission of women? The men said they were only passing along the pastor's teachings, yet, at the same time, some male Church members inflicted suffering onto their wives, such as adultery or physical or emotional violence. How could the pastor equate male privileges with extra-marital affairs? I could not understand it, but I knew of this because my then-husband formed part of the men's ministry and had shared these male leaders' beliefs.

I do believe a pastor should have authority under the name of Jesus Christ and use his word and wisdom to address these issues at Church. But any admonition should address the seriousness of a sin—not just be used as a reason to demean women. So while the pastor said that women's gossip was the culprit of our sin, instead, I felt that wives' needs were never addressed. And instead, many women—myself included—felt misunderstood and suffered in silence.

I was struggling with all this when I got into a bad car accident that August. I had just picked up John, who was two months old at the time, from Cristy's home. She watched him while we worked. Charles had washed and vacuumed my car over the weekend and had not put the car seat back in correctly. I was in a rush. I didn't get off work until 5:00 p.m.; then I had to get John and race home in time to cook dinner because Charles liked it served at 7:00 p.m. during the week. I started making a left turn at the gated front entrance to our apartment complex and failed to yield to a big truck, which crashed into the passenger side of the car.

I must have passed out, but I remember some people taking me to sit under a tree. I was so scared I was literally shaking. I thought I'd killed my son. He had been thrown from the car seat and trapped under the glove compartment on the passenger side. The firefighters had to use a special tool to pry open the front passenger door and extract him. Luckily, neither of us was injured. That accident created a fear of driving so deep that I started having panic attacks whenever I drove.

I quit the Dallas Dusters job while I recovered emotionally; then, that November, my former supervisor recruited me to work at Merry Maids, which was expanding. We worked in teams of two women, and I soon ascended to the role of team captain, meaning I was in charge of the other woman on my team. There were times when we knocked out two to three homes a day. However, the hard work was putting a strain on me physically, especially on my lower back. I was also doing a lot of driving, much of it on freeways in heavy traffic, which I hated, and my anxiety began creeping up.

Before too long, I had to tell the owner that I preferred to be a second team partner so I did not have to drive, which is how I got teamed up with Margaret, an older, compassionate woman who was a grandmotherly figure to me. She soon became a good friend, someone I could confide in. She would bring me books to read and buy me coffee, all those things a grandma does. It was the first time I'd experienced such kind, tender maternal love from a stranger. One day, we finished our first job and discovered the next one had been canceled, so she invited me to her home for lunch. I cherished that time with her. Margaret was truly heaven sent, a kind soul who lifted me up.

She also wanted to have me over for dinner so I could meet her husband, and even offered to drive me back to our apartment afterward. My avoidance of driving was so bad at this point that Charles picked me up at the Merry Maids office every day at 5:00 p.m. after Margaret dropped me off. I didn't tell Charles about her dinner invitation, because I knew he wouldn't want me to go. He'd become so deeply involved with his church that he did not like me to spend time with anyone but other church members. And I just could not bear another lecture from him about the doctrine on submission that his church espoused.

We still had some happy moments, though. That Christmas, we took John to Mexico to visit Charles's parents so they could meet their grandson. It was also my first time meeting them. Their village was small and humble but rich in tradition. The whole extended family came together for Christmas dinner, singing carols and exchanging gifts, an experience surpassing anything I'd known before in my short life. The last time I'd been in Mexico, it had been nothing but pain. It felt right that I'd returned with Charles and was now surrounded by nothing but love.

***

Being on speaking terms with my mom meant I could finally have Daddy Lou and my brothers back in my life. They'd come over when we hosted holidays or family barbecues, or we'd go to their home when it was their turn.

My relationship with my mom was still strained. I hadn't reached the point of forgiving her yet, not just for the trauma of my childhood but for what she'd done to Daddy Lou by having an affair, though I was trying. She'd since stopped seeing her lover, something she'd confessed to me a few months prior, but not nearly enough time had passed yet for those wounds to heal. I'd started to accept that my mom would always be mentally unstable, but I couldn't stay away from her for long. I still found myself desperate for her approval and love whenever she was around.

At times, our dysfunctional family tree drew us together as much as it tore us apart. Over and over, various family members—myself included—couldn't say no when one of us was in need (and it took me years to learn how to break out of that cycle). I was about to experience this once again when an old family member came back into my life.

When I was a child, my mother's cousin, Allison, and her husband would invite us to family get-togethers. Her daughters were nice and always had a lot of everything—food, clothes, toys. I remember them having all these freestanding clothes racks overflowing with pretty outfits, and once, after hearing my mother chastise me for something, Allison told me to go pick out whatever I wanted. I treasured those family get-togethers at her home, so when I saw her for the first time in more than a decade, when she showed up to my mother's Easter cookout in 1986, I was thrilled. Allison had a certain magnetism about her. She was beautiful, with dark hair and a warm smile.

For the next year, I saw her off and on when she came into town and learned more about what was going on in her life. So much of what she told me resonated. Much like me, Allison had known trauma, heartache, and abuse. She said she felt trapped in a prison, that her husband would make demand after demand and force her to give in to his sexual advances, which was only deepening the resentment she already felt toward him. But he was a good provider. He'd become a plumber, and on the side, they sold antique furniture she bought at estate sales in upscale neighborhoods and local flea markets.

In November 1986, she left her husband and children and moved to Garland with her boyfriend, Jerry. I knew she was looking for a job, so, wanting to repay her for all she'd done for me as a child, I got her one at Merry Maids.

At first, Allison was a hard worker. New employees were in training for the first thirty days, and Allison was assigned to my team. She was supposed to shadow us and observe and perform the lesser chores like vacuuming and taking out the trash. One day, about two weeks after she started, she told me she was going to take out the trash—but she never came back. I let my team captain know, and she called the office right away and spoke to the owner, who called the homeowner and asked her to come home and check her belongings.

After we finished, Margaret told me she had to go drop me off at Merry Maids because the owner wanted to speak with me. I panicked. I wouldn't be formally diagnosed with post-traumatic stress disorder (PTSD) until 1989, but after my kidnapping and the repeated sexual abuse, all my symptoms—a racing heart, anxiety—would frequently kick in. Once I arrived, a receptionist told me to go into the owner's wife's private office. It turned out that the homeowner suspected Allison had taken off with a very expensive diamond necklace, and they were threatening to call the police. While my own performance with the company was extraordinary, I was beyond embarrassed. I knew stealing was common in our family. My uncles were in prison serving long-term sentences for burglary and aggravated assault. Despite all that, Allison had needed help, and I'd vouched for her. I started crying. The owner's wife called the client and was finally able to persuade them to give us three days to get that necklace back. The owner's wife told the client she'd pay for the necklace if we couldn't recover it.

When I tracked down Allison, she confessed and profusely apologized. She told me her boyfriend, Jerry, was a junkie and that she too was doing drugs. I was shocked, but luckily Allison gave up the diamond necklace. She said she did it because she loved me. I felt so helpless. Allison had embarrassed me, but she was suffering, and I knew so well the soul-crushing shame that she was feeling. It seemed to have a hold on her and me both, stemming from our childhood traumas and our dysfunctional family.

Allison was fired but thankfully was not arrested. I was sad, but we stayed in touch. After he found out about the stolen necklace, Charles didn't want me spending time with her, but I rebelled and went out dancing with Allison several weekends in a row. I was young and thin and didn't lack for male attention, which I needed more desperately than ever as I tried to deal with another failing marriage.

One night, when we had snuck out to a dance club, Allison confessed to me that she wasn't just doing crack, cocaine, and heroin—she was addicted to them. I'd gone outside and found her with a man trying to get her to have sex with him in exchange for drugs. I'd pulled her inside the dance club, then taken her to a local Waffle House, where Allison shared the story of her addiction. I tried to talk her into getting help, but she said she was in too deep.

"What do you mean?" I asked her.

She said the man that had gotten her hooked would hunt her down if she tried to flee. Allison shared she had been frequenting bars and would offer sex in exchange for money.

She told me she had worked the corners in Corpus Christi, her hometown. Agnes, her mother and my grandma's biological sister, had passed on to Allison the pattern of turning to sex work when times got hard. Allison had fallen prey to the streets. She told me how working in both major and minor cities is rough for women, especially in Texas. Drugs, alcohol, and sex work had become her way of life, she said bitterly. She wept for the family she'd abandoned. Her children chastised, humiliated, and shamed her for leaving their father. I could see that she thought her fate was sealed. Perhaps she felt she was paying for the sins of other generations; her mother had killed two men but never served a day in prison. Agnes had told police she killed them in self-defense because they beat her and exploited her sexually, which I have no doubt is true, but the burden of their deaths still weighed heavily on her and the family. Allison's words touched my heart, and I will never forget that conversation.

Allison eventually reconciled with her husband, and after that, we lost touch again. Many years later, in 2003, Allison was found dead of a heroin overdose beside the railroad tracks. She'd lost the battle with her demons.

Allison had mourned the loss of her sons and daughters; their lack of forgiveness had driven her to the pits of despair. I guess the pain had been too much for her, and death had come looking for her too soon. Allison had been a warrior and fierce protector, but no longer. Some of her children, perhaps regretting their estrangement, held a memorial vigil and for the longest time would often bring flowers to an open field near where she'd been found. I wish I could have attended her funeral, but my husband at the time wouldn't allow it, saying she'd only received what was just. I cannot accept this. No one had understood her pain more than I. I had bonded with her as a sister.

I hate that Allison died such a lonely, sad death. We should never judge another soul. We never know what their journey has been, what struggles they've had, and how hard they've tried to overcome them. Allison had tried and failed, like so many in our family, and I cannot fault her for that. I knew that her path could so easily have been mine.

***

Over the next year, Charles and I continued to clash over the restrictions the church placed on its members, and by June 1988, it was clear our marriage was in free fall.

All this subtle but very present control had placed me in permanent panic mode: I sensed that I was being coerced and did not agree with the strictures, but I often ended up giving in just to feel accepted—my need to please, to earn acceptance and love, made me an easy target. Looking back, I wonder if the issue wasn't so much the church as it was my own wounds and emotional immaturity. Something inside me felt that I didn't deserve the happiness of a stable, normal family. All that buried bitterness, shame, guilt, and resentment kept my inner demons well nourished, and over time, I started to chafe against the bonds of my marriage. My family felt more like a burden than a source of joy. Those old familiar cravings for more love and affection that had sent me looking for other men while I was with Cesar came crawling back. Charles and I started to argue more.

As I was trying to sort through all these conflicting emotions, my aunt Nina, my mother's youngest sister, came to visit with her three children. She had just separated from her abusive, alcoholic husband and wanted to move back to the Dallas area. We had a lot in common. She too had married at age fifteen and never had a chance at a normal adolescence. We connected, as I still felt some resentment about that loss in my own life. I'd dated a bit between Cesar and Charles, but by this point, it felt like I'd spent more of my life in a relationship than out of one. Now I was a mom and had to be an adult; I would never get that chance to go back and be an innocent kid.

The same weekend Nina arrived, Charles went on a men's retreat through his church. I didn't realize at the time that he'd gone to ask for marriage advice from his church's deacons. Even when he wasn't in the house, he was working to make our relationship better. I, on the other hand, used this time away from Charles to go back on the prowl. Nina hired a sitter for the kids, and we went out to the dance halls together and had the time of our lives. Nina loved doing all the things that weren't allowed by Charles's church. She wore makeup and revealing clothes, smoked, and drank beer. She wasn't a good role model, but Nina did all the things I thought I wanted to be free to do myself. Maybe if I'd been more emotionally mature, I would have seen that I was playing out the same behaviors I'd seen from my mom. I was still angry with her for cheating on Daddy Lou, yet here I was, ready to do the same thing to Charles.

That night at the dance hall, I met Gerardo. He was handsome, with dark reddish-brown hair, about the same height as Charles. But, at nineteen, he was just a few months younger than me—much closer to my age than Charles. Like me, he'd come from a broken home. His dad had been murdered when he was eight, and his mom had abandoned him and his siblings, running away with an alcoholic. Gerardo had been raised by his grandparents, but they'd given him little in the way of love and affection. His scars and wounds were so close to my own that I couldn't help but be drawn to him. And we had a physical attraction to each other too; I was young and pretty, eager for his attention, and Gerardo was more than willing to make a move on me.

When Charles got home from his weekend retreat, he found a photo Gerardo and I had taken of ourselves at the dance hall and confronted me. I told him Gerardo was just a friend, but he didn't believe me. I finally confessed I'd slept with Gerardo that night. Charles was devastated. Our arguments grew more intense, a deep divide opening up between us where there had once been nothing but love. In the end, that love wasn't enough. Even throughout the best times with Charles, I had felt that void inside me, still craving a kind of love he wasn't able to give me. It wasn't his fault. He was a good man.

Charles struggled to forgive me, but in the end, he just couldn't; his church's strict doctrine forbade adultery. A week after he returned from the retreat, where he'd sought advice about how to save our marriage, he moved out of our apartment. I had been so happy when I'd met Charles, but our divorce became final in July 1989; our marriage had lasted only three short years, not even long enough for us to have that big ceremony he'd promised on our wedding night.

As for me, I was too hooked on my new relationship with Gerardo to pause and reflect on how things had gone so wrong so quickly.

PART TWO

1989 to 2015

7

The Past Keeps Coming Back

When I dove into my relationship with Gerardo to escape Charles's controlling ways, I thought I was running to my rescuer. It's no wonder—he played that role perfectly. He was so courteous and gallant. He truly swept me off my feet. I was flattered by the fact that he wanted to be so involved in every detail of my life. He walked me to the bathroom wherever we went; insisted on picking up the bill, even when grocery shopping; and was available to take me anywhere I wanted, even to a doctor's appointment. He would fend off other men at the dance halls and flash his gun to protect me as we walked to the car in the parking lot afterward. He didn't tell me what clothes to buy or wear. I was truly mesmerized by him, by all the attention he showered upon me. I felt safe and protected.

Though Charles and I had separated, he allowed John and me to stay in our apartment and agreed to pay my share of the rent for a few months. Nina and her three children moved into the second bedroom. We got by with rent money from Charles and the money Nina was able to contribute. Gerardo stayed with me every weekend. After a couple of months, though, Charles found out Gerardo had been sleeping over and told me I had to pay my own rent. At that point, I had no choice but to ask Gerardo for financial support. I was stuck between a rock and a hard place. I had no resources.

However, as soon as Gerardo began to provide financially for my son and me, he began to try to control me. It started small; for example, I had some white jean shorts that I absolutely loved. I thought I looked so cute in them, and I enjoyed the admiring looks I got from men when I wore them. But Gerardo didn't like me wearing them. One weekend, he came over and we went to the lake with my aunt and her kids while John went to church with his father and aunts. Gerardo was so attentive that weekend, assisting me with every detail. We were in the midst of a scorching heat wave that summer of August 1989, with temperatures soaring above one hundred degrees, so Gerardo decided to join Nina in drinking some cold beer while we were at the lake. That's the first time I saw the other side of Gerardo: his jealousy, which quickly turned to rage. He was angry that I was wearing those white shorts and attracting attention while I was at the lake.

We had an argument that night, a bad one. He started yelling and demanded that I take off my white shorts. I became frightened and obeyed him; when I did, Gerardo grabbed them and ripped them apart. Though I was now fearful of how he'd treat me, I allowed him to stay because I had no way to pay my rent. Once again, I'd allowed myself to get into a situation where I had no power. I was losing my autonomy, as I had with both Charles and Cesar, but I simply didn't know how to stop it. I was back to creating a dysfunctional, codependent relationship. I had no friends, and neither did Gerardo, which didn't help. We were each other's entire worlds.

Gerardo soon began criticizing Nina, saying she drank too much, that she was a whore and not fit to be a mother, and that she wasn't a good influence on me. He told me she needed to find a place of her own. When I tried to object, he pushed me against the bed and overpowered me with forced kisses.

I was frightened of Gerardo's anger. His voice would change, becoming forceful and threatening, which sent me into a panic. He would not physically hurt me, but he did hold my hands hard and tight and subdue me into having sex with him. When I tried to resist, Gerardo turned soft and affectionate until I complied with his wishes. It was not a healthy dynamic, and I knew that. But I told myself that he provided for us; having a man who took care of me financially made me feel secure. And in that way, I *was* happy. Before my divorce to Charles was finalized, I'd settled into the toxic relationship and was pregnant with my second son.

Gerardo and I were both thrilled with the prospect of a baby. Gerardo was on top of the world, becoming obsessed and overprotective. Though it was nice when he catered to my every need, he was critical and cruel all throughout my pregnancy, telling me I couldn't eat this or that, or that I was so fat the baby was likely to have heart problems. I had to report all the details from my checkups to him, and he never failed to make me feel guilty about something.

Our son Alan was born on a cold January day after I had been in labor for more than twenty hours. They'd given me too much medication in my epidural, and my legs had gone numb, and I couldn't push. Little Nikki emerged in the midst of the labor pain as Gerardo scolded me, telling me he wanted our son to be healthy and acting like the long labor was somehow my fault. I almost had to have an emergency C-section, but by the grace of God, Alan was born without one. Although healthy, he seemed nervous, as if the long labor had caused him a lot of distress. I do believe children can feel their mother's emotions while they're in the womb, and sometimes I wonder whether he could sense through my pregnancy that I lived with a lot of fear and anxiety.

Between holiday and birthday get-togethers, we'd go to Mom and Daddy Lou's for cookouts, because I felt such a need to see Daddy Lou, especially since Gerardo's drinking had been getting worse, and when he drank, he got angry. I felt so confused and, at times, angry myself, and Daddy Lou had always been my safe place. I could be in the worst mood, but when I arrived at their home, he could always make me smile. He called me Pipo, after a Spanish clown—a nickname he'd given me when I was growing up because I loved how clowns made sad children like me smile. I knew I was the apple of his eye, that he truly loved me as if I were his own daughter, because he told me that every time he saw me.

Daddy Lou had a chair beside the grill, and we'd all take turns sitting with him, seeking out his company and his advice. Even Gerardo. Daddy Lou always made sure to give me and the boys ten minutes of undivided attention. My favorite piece of chicken was the drumstick, so he cooked Mom's first, then mine. He was a doting grandfather to my boys, giving them cookies or blowing up balloons or filling water guns for them. Sometimes he even joined them in blowing bubbles.

Those cookouts were a welcome diversion for us all, though Gerardo still drove recklessly on the way home. He knew that driving erratically while drinking was one way to send me into a deep state of panic. He would make fun of me for being scared of driving home with him when he was drunk. And when he was sober the next day, he always denied all his cruel behavior.

I began to experience states of deep depression and anxiety, more intense than before. I'd also begun to struggle with my weight, something I'd never had to worry about in the past. Overeating made me feel good when everything else around me felt so bad. Still, on the outside, everything appeared stable, though I walked on pins and needles around Gerardo, trying not to say or do anything to upset him and provoke one of his hurtful, sarcastic remarks.

Yet our sons idolized him, seeing him as the perfect father. And for them, maybe he was. Gerardo took good care of all of us financially. He was a hard worker, he had a good manufacturing job with health insurance and a 401(k), and he got plenty of overtime. However, inside, I continued to fall apart. I felt so sad at times—and useless, because Gerardo did everything. I had no say in anything. Whenever I tried to speak up, Gerardo had a way of making fun of me, of criticizing me. It felt like I was once again living in captivity in Mexico with Cesar, and I began to regress. I had flashbacks, reliving some of my childhood trauma.

I soon began taking drives as a way to have some freedom and control. Because of my panic attacks, I started out by driving short distances. Gerardo even bought a second car I could use for transporting Alan and John, but he would not let me go anywhere without lecturing me about the dangers lurking outside the house. Still, driving began to bring me satisfaction and it helped me disconnect from the pressures of daily life.

Then Mom and Daddy Lou asked if we wanted to rent their other house. An opportunity had come up for my mother to buy the house next door to hers on a rent-to-own basis. So we became neighbors, and not surprisingly, it turned out that having Mom as our neighbor was not such a good idea. Hearing her voice always gave me anxiety. It was as if I still feared her rejection.

One summer day, Amy came from Brownsville, Texas, to visit Julie. She was so different from my mother, so warm and loving that I sometimes had trouble believing they were actually related. I'd stayed in touch with her after I'd left home and would take the boys down to South Padre Island Beach in Brownsville to visit her once a year. They adored her. My aunt was a gracious hostess. She always welcomed us with open arms, cooked homemade meals for us, and seemed to enjoy the quality family time we spent together. Every two years or so, she'd come to visit us and stay with my mother.

On this particular day, Alan and John had seen Amy sitting with my mom on her front porch and asked if they could go see her. I looked out the big picture window in my small home and saw them myself, so I told the boys they could go say hi. When they came back later, their little faces were sad, and they said, "Mom, Grandma said we need to come home, that you should be caring for us." This hurt me deeply, that my mother would get so angry at my precious boys just for coming over and saying hi to Aunt Amy. But I decided to just move past the incident. The following day, Amy knocked on the front door of our small wood-frame home. A few minutes later, my mother popped in, as if nothing had happened. She always got under my skin when she came over uninvited—which she frequently did, since she owned the house we were renting—but I never said anything to her about it. It is something I cannot explain. As a child, she had instilled so much fear in me that I was always anxious around her and then angry that I could never voice those feelings I had bottled up for years.

Because of Mom's mental disorders, I never knew what

to expect, how she'd react. She could go from being pleasant and agreeable to being filled with rage in the blink of an eye. It was like a switch flipped in her. I still desperately wanted her to love me, though at this point, I don't think I believed that was even possible. I'd bought her expensive perfumes, designer purses, and jewelry, hoping she would give me a little bit of love, but all I'd gotten were fake-happy smiles in return. She didn't have a strong support system where she could work through her inner demons, like a place of worship or a therapist. I worried that she would always struggle with her mental health if she didn't make some drastic changes in her life.

Not too long after that incident, Gerardo and I decided to move out of Mom's rental home. We really wanted a place for our sons to grow up and be as happy and as healthy as they could—which meant being far away from Mom. We wanted to buy our very first home someday and were saving money for a down payment, but we weren't there yet, so we decided to rent again. We got a one-year lease for a small two-bedroom cottage with a huge tree-filled backyard big enough for the boys to have a swing set.

It was in this rental cottage that I found out I was pregnant again. This turned out to be bittersweet, because I miscarried not long after that. I was so sad, and when Gerardo picked me up from Baylor Hospital afterward, he did not say anything about the loss of our baby. It was as if he didn't care. His lack of emotion deeply wounded me. How could he feel nothing after such a devastating loss? Who was this man I had committed to? I sank deeper and deeper into a pool of depression.

I got pregnant again quickly, just three months later. I'd shed a lot of tears over my miscarriage, but I felt blessed to be expecting a child again. It was as if my tears had reached heaven. The news came in early February 1993 after a home pregnancy test, and I was so filled with joy. In the midst of sadness and despair, we had been blessed.

I began going to my OB-GYN appointments, which meant I was doing a lot more driving. They say emotional driving increases your chances of having an accident tenfold, and with the pregnancy hormones raging in my body, I was more emotional than ever. With two small children, I was always in a hurry, trying to do too many things at once.

One day, as I was heading to a doctor's appointment, a car came out of nowhere and slammed into my truck when Alan was with me. Luckily, we both had relatively minor injuries. But then a few months later, a car rear-ended me when Art and I were taking Robert to work. This time, the truck was totaled, and I sustained multiple neck and spine injuries and developed bulging discs in my lower back. After that, my fear of driving became a full-blown phobia, so I stopped altogether, and Gerardo had to take me to my physical therapy sessions.

But something good did come from the accident, a blessing in disguise. I received a $20,000 lump-sum pain-and-suffering settlement, and we were finally able to buy our very first home. I was so excited. I remember searching for homes, one after the other, until we found the perfect one. It was a brick cottage with a good-sized backyard and lush landscaping, and it was within walking distance of the elementary schools. It truly captured my heart. Our real estate agent, Mr. Fleischman, was a nice man who became sort of a father figure to me as well as a friend. He began to show Gerardo and me how the real estate business worked and helped us by representing us in the real estate transaction.

Gerardo continued to make all the decisions relating to the household—repairs, furniture, and any of our other needs.

Perhaps as a passive-aggressive way of rebelling, I began to develop unhealthy spending habits. I started to receive catalogs for Fingerhut, JCPenney, and other stores and purchased things from them with credit cards I'd acquired. I loved the rush of happiness spending gave me. I was able to keep it hidden from Gerardo because I got the mail every day. But it wasn't long before he noticed that we did not have any money and wanted to know where it had gone. I finally had to tell him because I had to dip into our savings to pay off some of my credit cards. I was starting to understand how my bad choices, one after the other, had consequences, and it made me bitter. But I also realized that, for the sake of the child I was carrying, I had to remain well, so I tried to stay focused on that. Eventually I bore a healthy eight-pound baby boy, whom we called Junior, via C-section. After his birth, I again noticed Gerardo's lack of emotional attachment to him, yet I also knew he took care of our boys, protecting them as best he could.

During this time, I tried to appreciate all that I had. I had come a long way from that scared, abused child, and while it was far from perfect, I knew I was lucky in so many ways. Gerardo and I had two beautiful sons and a beautiful home, and while John lived with his father, Charles, he was able to stay with us every other weekend. At times we felt like the perfect family, and I couldn't understand why I felt so empty and broken, which then only underscored and deepened those feelings of inadequacy. I knew Gerardo and I lacked true intimacy, but I also realized we both came from broken homes and each carried our own baggage into the relationship.

Then, in October 1993, my grandmother paid us a surprise visit, and what she had to say changed everything I thought I knew about my own life.

We hadn't seen my grandmother in five years. She looked frail, smaller somehow. She'd been diagnosed with pulmonary hypertension (she had been a heavy smoker for many years) and was using an oxygen tank, so she didn't travel much. My aunt Lori, one of my mother's sisters, had dropped her off at our home, then went to get something to eat so we could talk privately. My grandmother knew her health was failing, so maybe she was worried that she would die and I'd never know the truth.

When she saw me holding Junior, she asked, "Has your mom stopped by to visit you and the baby?"

"Just barely," I responded.

Grandma began to weep and asked for a cup of coffee. Her voice was soft, and her face was pale and appeared frail as she asked Gerardo to sit beside me. She told my husband and me that she was going to tell me something that would help me understand my mom's anger toward me. She began by saying life is fragile, that she knew my mother had never allowed me to get close to her and she knew why, that she wanted to rid herself of this secret she'd been keeping for so many years. Then she revealed that I was a child of rape; that Julie had tried to give me up for adoption to an affluent family, had been about to sign the papers when my grandmother had convinced her to keep me, saying she would raise me instead. But my mother had decided to raise me herself.

It all began to make sense, how my mother had rejected me for as long as I could remember. Now I knew why; my very existence was a daily reminder of the trauma she'd gone through. Rather than deal with her own feelings of regret, guilt, or anger, Mom had taken it out on me. She'd come to resent me—her own daughter—as much as she resented my biological father for raping her.

Still, I felt for her. She too had been rejected and abused as a child. She had repeated the only style of parenting she knew, even though it was the same parenting behavior that had pained and tormented her. Intellectually I understood this, but the effect was still devastating. How could I expect anyone else to love me when my own mother didn't?

By the time Lori returned to our home, I was sobbing, saying, "I don't have anyone." This led to another devastating revelation. My grandmother told me that my father had sought me out when I was four or five years old, but my mother had refused to let him see me. It was a lot to take in.

Afterward, my grandmother swore us to secrecy. She feared my mother's wrath, so she made me promise I wouldn't reveal what I knew about my parentage until after she was dead. She seemed calmer after she told me; perhaps she felt more at peace now that she'd unburdened herself. But I was in turmoil. The hardest part was knowing that Grandma had had to beg Mom to keep me. This was shattering—even as it explained so much about how my mother had treated me.

Once again, my emotions began to spiral out of control. The dark clouds began to form.

***

The one thing that wasn't complicated in my life was motherhood, so I did my best to focus on that in the wake of my grandmother's revelations, though inwardly I was struggling with all the emotions she'd stirred up. I found true joy in raising my children. Junior was a good baby who slept through the night at an early age, unlike Alan, who as an infant had been a little more anxious and would wake up every two hours crying with colic and other worrisome things. At this point,

John lived with us full time, only visiting his father every other weekend and during the summer holidays.

The demands of mothering three boys were a lot to handle, though I was filled with happiness as I watched them grow into themselves. John was in elementary school, and our home was just one block away, so, since there were school crossing guards, I felt comfortable letting him walk to and from school by himself. Alan was very much into video games. His favorite console was the Nintendo 64, and his best-loved games were the Super Mario games. He was such a bright young child. He would get one game after another, and by God, this child would challenge himself and beat those games, which kept him busy during the day. And Junior was happy to play in his crib or toddle around in his walker, playing with his toys. I tried my best to be a good mother to our children. I'd read to my boys since they were young, and I introduced them to the library when they were old enough to read. I wanted them to go to college, to have all the opportunities I never had.

On the outside, it seemed like I had everything, certainly more than I had ever had in my own dysfunctional childhood. Yet I was always very anxious, because inside, I was lonely and unhappy, and Little Nikki emerged more frequently. Though I'd given Gerardo two sons, all he could do was criticize my parenting, which shattered my self-esteem. My mom and Daddy Lou were still hosting regular family cookouts, which I truly enjoyed attending so I could spend time with Daddy Lou. I didn't get to speak to him as much as I'd have liked because my mother kept him busy catering to her whims. I'd become even more estranged from my mother after Grandma had revealed her secret to me, but I could not bear to stay away from Daddy Lou or keep my children from seeing him. So I kept my distance when we went, speaking to my mother as little as possible.

My half brothers David and Robert were now grown men in their midtwenties. Art was twenty-one. Ronald, the youngest, was eleven. I loved all of them. I cherished those get-togethers at Mom's home because they were about the only times I socialized with my brothers or saw Daddy Lou; Mom had become Daddy Lou's caretaker three years prior, in 1991, after he'd injured his spinal column at work. Although he got disability income through social security, it wasn't enough to cover the bills, so my mother had to work. My brothers helped out, but David and Robert had both gotten married, and each had their own families and financial obligations. And my other two half brothers were too young to contribute. Still, those were happy times.

My sons were thriving too. Gerardo always made time for them, whether it was helping them assemble their toys, attending their plays, or going to meet-the-teacher nights. In fact, the main reason we decided to make our relationship official that October was for them. Gerardo had been raised Catholic and wanted our sons to be baptized, which meant we had to get married. It was a simple ceremony at Good Shepherd Catholic Church in Garland, which we'd attended off and on. Nina, David, and his fiancée were the witnesses. There were no other guests; there was no reception, no tossing of the bouquet, no romantic first dance. I didn't even have an engagement ring or a traditional wedding dress. Instead, Nina bought me a white suit to wear.

I'd begun to see a psychologist again because I'd been struggling with resentment toward my mother since finding out that she had wanted to give me up for adoption and that

I was a child of rape. And I still harbored some resentment toward Gerardo as well. The unhappier I was, the more money I spent, and we were getting deeper and deeper into debt. I was so naive that fast-talking sales agents would sometimes trick me. I loved jewelry and would let myself get talked into buying something with a loan through a financer or at low-end jewelry stores. One woman managed to sell me about $1,500 worth of gold jewelry in just under fifteen minutes. It was low-quality 10K gold, and when combined with the other debt, it put me in way over my head.

By early 1995, I was determined to get myself out of the debt we were in, so every Saturday I would ask Gerardo to take us to estate sales in the Highland Park area, an upscale neighborhood near Dallas. I began buying used merchandise and furniture, then holding monthly garage sales. I took the only skill I had, which was bargaining, and learned to make a profit by buying low and selling high. I stayed up all night pricing clothing and toys that the boys no longer played with and sanding and staining the furniture so I could resell it. I soon developed repeat clientele who wanted me to refurbish their furniture. Others came to me looking for appliances. I went without sleep for days, placing stickers on the items I was selling and putting them in boxes, trying desperately to get out of some of the debt that I had racked up.

Gerardo attacked me, blamed me, and accused me of mishandling money. He told me the only thing I was good at was being a housewife. I was ashamed of my role in accumulating our debt, but when Gerardo would say something about it to me, I'd lash out at him instead of acknowledging what I'd done. I wanted us to figure a way out of it together, and I didn't see the point in assigning blame. I should have said all that to him, but instead, to get back at him, I made him carry the heavy pieces of furniture and set up the tables for the garage sales. I soon tired of the endless and difficult work, though, and gave up the garage sales. My credit had taken such a dive, and we were being hounded by so many collection agencies, that it no longer mattered. Instead, I kept spending. I wanted my boys to have vacations, so I found a way to take them to Six Flags, SeaWorld, and South Padre Beach to see Aunt Amy. Those were the best days, the best summers.

While some things were good, trouble was always just beneath the surface. I began experiencing sudden mood swings, irritability, and anger, coupled with severe anxiety. Whenever Mom was around, I'd get depressed and lose interest in things. Then there were days when I would have an excessive desire for sex, at times reenacting things Cesar had done to me. Sometimes Gerardo was the initiator. Other times, I would also reenact other abuses that had happened to me. It was my way of getting some control in my marriage and of trying to get some type of deep emotional reaction from Gerardo, because there was no foreplay, no intimacy, no hugs, no kisses, no appreciation for the pure act of love between us anymore.

Yet outside the bedroom, Gerardo sometimes could be kind, even generous, giving me extra spending money, asking if I needed help with chores, taking the boys to the park. These small, subtle, seemingly insignificant things he did would confuse me, especially in contrast with the dark anger and lack of emotional connection he generally displayed.

I still had no real female friends, with the exception of one young lady named Krissy. She was a Jehovah's Witness and would leave booklets at our home. I began to read them, until one day, after several months of this, she asked if I could join her for a cup of coffee. I told her I did not have a car, and she offered to take me to the McDonald's close to where we lived.

December was always a hard month for me. It's a time for families and love, but it just reminded me of what I didn't have, in my childhood and even now.

Junior was attending pre-K four hours a day, and Alan was in first grade all day, so I accepted her invitation. I spoke to Krissy about my abusive childhood. She was sympathetic. She shared with me too, telling me about her husband, who had a business with his dad and that she enjoyed giving time to the community. I kept our friendship a secret from Gerardo.

But my mood swings were still there, lurking beneath the surface, and that January, I became angry and full of rage, an indication that my emotions and Gerardo's lack of them were taking a toll. I was a wilted flower, but I was ready to fight. The next-door neighbor's children liked to play baseball in our front yard, and I began running them off, asking them to stop. One day, their mother came out to speak with me, and I got angry and slammed the door in her face. This became the start of an uncomfortable situation. Things worsened, and I demanded that we sell the house and move. I told Gerardo it was either that or I was going to leave him.

My friendship with Krissy had begun to empower me. I now knew about social programs and transitional housing for domestic violence victims. Gerardo was reluctant to sell our home, and in one of my anxiety attacks, I blurted out, "I know I can get a place to stay. I know where to go for help. I have a friend who will help me."

Suddenly Gerardo looked at me—he knew he could easily play with my mind—and said, "My love, I know you have been struggling with the neighbor, and I don't want you to be angry. I don't want you to be under such stress." Gerardo could quickly disguise himself as a considerate man, and this confused me, as I so desperately wanted to believe he was a caring husband.

Gerardo told me to call the real estate agent who helped us buy our first home and tell him to put our house on the market, which is what I did. I knew he was experienced, and I trusted him. When we met with him, I asked him how much our home was worth and discovered we would actually walk away with a small lump sum if we sold it, because we had some equity. I proposed sprucing it up with fresh paint and new landscaping to up the numbers, and he praised me for my negotiation skills. This is how I discovered I had a passion for real estate and wondered if it was something I might consider doing.

Gerardo belittled me, saying, "How do you think you'll ever be an agent? You need an education to become a real estate agent. You need a piece of paper called a degree." That killed my dream—and my enthusiasm.

At least for the time being.

***

Gerardo said I could buy whatever home I wanted, as long as it was within our price range. To prepare our old home, he painted the inside and did some landscaping, like I'd suggested, and we sold it above the asking price in record time. We actually had several offers. We soon found a darling new home in Sachse, a suburb not far from Dallas. The year was 1997.

I hadn't forgotten about Krissy, though. She'd been doing some missionary work, and I hadn't seen her for a while. Then she stopped by our new house. She came in, and I began to weep. Krissy was my only true friend, and despite the move being a barrier to our ability to get together, I didn't want to lose her. We agreed we would keep in contact, but as soon as she'd gone, something told me I wouldn't see her again. Today, I can clearly see how Gerardo manipulated me by agreeing to sell our house and move. He'd known I'd felt empowered when I had first mentioned her and all the help I could get as an abuse victim, so he'd made sure to sever our friendship. Krissy had been a true threat to Gerardo. He was not about to let me go—or stop controlling me.

8

Love, Family, and Real Estate

As we settled into our new home and the boys began school, I was lonely once again. Depression started to take root again.

The boys began making friends, and while I became friends with one of their moms, I wasn't adapting well to living in Sachse. By the end of 1997, my depression was worsening to the point that I started seeing a therapist again once every two weeks. He put me on Prozac and Valium, which made me feel like a zombie.

Meanwhile, Gerardo was drinking a six-pack every two to three days when he got home from work, and we were drifting further apart than ever. He was under a lot of pressure with his manufacturing job, which demanded a lot of overtime, but he wouldn't talk to me about it. Gerardo had told me that he trusted no one, that he'd learned to take care of himself when he was eight years old, when his mother had sent him and his three siblings to live with their grandparents after his father had been murdered. He said that he was dead inside. I believed him.

Maybe his abandonment issues were why he wanted to be involved in every aspect of our sons' lives. He did not allow Alan to join a soccer team because he could get injured, he said. I believe this caused stress and anxiety in Alan. I had noticed he was beginning to show signs of withdrawal, not from his education but rather from areas of his social life. I tried to talk to Gerardo about this, but he told me he wanted his family to have the best that life could offer. And he wanted to keep us safe.

I got more and more frustrated with him. Gerardo did not want our sons to have chores. Instead, he would come home from work and wash dishes or cook on days that I was just not up to it because of my depression. I vented all my frustrations to Alan. He became my confidant, which was a mistake; I should never have placed such a burden on him. I was clinging to him because I had no one else to confide in. No parent should ever do that to a child.

It was wrong of me, and I deeply regret it.

***

It seems I could never get along with neighbors. I had a very low tolerance for frustration. Rather than standing up to fear, I had begun to feel fear was controlling me instead. As the boys grew older—Alan was nine, Junior was six, and John was fourteen—one of our next-door neighbors in Sachse moved out, and a family with untrained pit bulls and unruly teens moved in. Their dogs dug holes underneath our fence, and their children trespassed on our property, even spray-painting the fence. I was worried the dogs would come onto our property and I was upset about the defacing, so I tried to talk to the neighbors about it. I was angry and reactive and told them I would call the police on them. The teens vandalized Gerardo's car afterward, and my anxiety was at an all-time high.

That was the final straw. I asked Gerardo if we could sell our home and move back to Garland. After he agreed, I called our real estate agent and asked if he could find us something, anything, even a rent-to-own property. We'd finally filed for Chapter 13 bankruptcy in September 1996, which had allowed us to restructure our $32,000 of debt, but I hadn't realized you had to keep making payments, and after I skipped one to buy Christmas presents, we'd fallen behind once again. As a result, both our credit scores were severely affected. That blessed man found us a great home that was unbelievably perfect. It had three bedrooms and two baths and a nonqualifying assumable mortgage, which was a loan that was popular back in the 1980s and '90s because there were no income or credit requirements.

The agent told the owner, a schoolteacher, that we had a financial situation that required a few years to get a good credit status. Though she was asking at least $6,000 more than we could afford for the down payment, Mr. Fleischman let us borrow $3,000 on a secured second-lien note, thus helping us sell our current home and place the larger down payment on the home in Garland. We officially moved into our new home in September 1999.

Two months later, Gerardo's estranged mother called him, asking if two of her sons—Roland, who was sixteen, and Fernie, who was nineteen—could come live with us. She wanted them to have a better life than they could have in Mexico, where they now lived. Gerardo agreed and converted the garage into a bedroom for them. By Thanksgiving, they had arrived.

Roland was very shy and quiet but well mannered. Fernie was bolder and more confident. I felt an instant connection with him as soon as our eyes met when he walked into our home. They'd been traveling for more than a day and a half, barely eating, and they were hungry, so I prepared them mole, a traditional Mexican dish with chicken, served with Spanish rice, that is generally made for special occasions like birthdays, weddings, baptisms, and so forth. Fernie offered to help me wash the dishes and clean up after dinner—and that was on day one. I was literally blushing.

But Gerardo quickly told Fernie to leave the kitchen alone, insisting that he would help me. He did not like another man offering to help his wife, even though he had not ever let our boys assist me with the dishes or household chores either, which was typical of his machismo behavior. Much of Gerardo's day-to-day behavior exemplified the traits commonly associated with machismo culture. I felt hurt by his possessive, controlling nature and his demands for subservience.

As Fernie and Roland settled into our new home in Garland, they both secured construction jobs through other family members who lived in the area. Because Fernie drove machinery for his construction job, he didn't work on rainy days. Gerardo was at work, the boys were at school, so sometimes it was just Fernie and me spending time together. Despite our twelve-year age difference—he was nineteen years old to my thirty-one—we had common interests and good communication. Most of all, he offered me sympathy. He still volunteered to help me clean and cook, something Gerardo only did when he wanted something from me, like anal sex. We became best friends, but we never committed adultery. I'd been unfaithful while married to my Charles, and I did not want to hurt anyone anymore. Instead, I let Fernie care for me when he saw my emotional suffering. "Why do you stay in this relationship?" he'd often ask me. Or he'd say, "My half brother has no heart." Fernie had witnessed domestic violence committed against his mom, and he was able to sympathize with my situation. In addition, his words met actions—he was such a caring, honest young man. I'd never experienced such kind acts of service, such as having help with groceries.

By January 2000, I realized I was in love with Fernie. Our relationship was based on true affinity, trust, friendship, and respect. Fernie always respected me as a woman, never taking advantage of my poor mental and emotional well-being, but we were doomed, destined to be star-crossed lovers.

Alan and Junior seemed to really care for him, although they were too young to fully understand the situation. My oldest son, John, was cold and indifferent to him. Maybe John suspected what was starting to happen between Fernie and me. Fernie bought me a card and small gifts, and I told him to stop. By now we both knew we had strong feelings for each other. The following week, we had a daylong conversation about that and what we were up against. He asked me to divorce Gerardo. I was torn, but we could not deny that we had fallen in love. I hired an attorney, and Fernie helped me pay for it. Boy, was I in for a shock. Gerardo was not going to let me go that easily.

After I confessed to Gerardo that I had fallen in love with his half brother, he called me a whore, a slut. He followed me to the patio of our home, where I'd fled to escape his yelling. We were arguing, and he pushed me to the ground, subdued me, and told me he was going to find his brother and hurt or kill him. He left me feeling not only guilty but emotionally and mentally confused. As always, he made me doubt myself and any decisions I made. But this time, things also turned physically violent. Gerardo kicked me and dragged me to the ground, putting pressure on the back of my neck while I suffocated on the grass.

I had him served with divorce papers while he was at work, and by March 2000 we were formally divorced. I asked Gerardo to move out of our home. The next months were pure chaos. Gerardo was enraged and determined to crush me. I lived in a state of panic, fear, and anxiety. I was terrified that Gerardo would kill me or Fernie, as he had threatened to do, so Fernie moved in with one of his uncles in a close-by suburb. He would call me from work to check up on me and the boys. He was a true gentleman. I wish Gerardo had been like that.

I received a lump sum of Gerardo's pension plan and placed a down payment on a rent-to-own home in Mesquite that I moved into with the boys. We decided that Fernie would live separately from us because of Gerardo's constant harassment, but I was determined to break free of Gerardo's abuse and become independent.

During this time, Fernie's unconditional love kept me grounded. We shared a pure love. We gave the best of ourselves in our intimacy, which was beautiful and passionate yet tender and loving, and he met my needs emotionally. For the first time in years, I felt like a true woman. On Mother's Day, Fernie proposed to me. He even bought me a lovely simple ring, but it was the gift of unconditional love and respect he gave me that truly mattered. I married him in October 2000. This enraged Gerardo, who terrorized us. He broke into the house several times and accused Fernie of stealing his wife and his family. Had I been stronger, I would have had Gerardo arrested or obtained a restraining order against him.

Instead, in late December, I began to look for an attorney to divorce Fernie, because my fear that Gerardo might hurt him or even me was overpowering everything that was good in my life. We'd been married such a short time; I was able to get it annulled in less than forty-five days.

After the annulment, Gerardo moved back in, and we were soon living in the house in Garland again. Gerardo resented the fact that the home in Mesquite was an accomplishment I'd attained all on my own. He made me break the lease on the beautiful brick home, insisting that Alan and Junior were unhappy in the Mesquite school district. I felt ashamed. Somehow he'd always been able to crush me with his cruel, cold words. Though we didn't get remarried, he'd convinced me to give him a second chance, saying my boys would grow up hating me, that he would fight for sole custody of them. I'd agreed to reconcile with him for their sake.

As much as it broke my heart, I cut off contact with Fernie. To this day, I can truly say Fernie was a gift of love from God. During some very dark moments I was facing, he was a bright light. In many ways, God was present and protecting me. Grace wins time after time.

***

Over the next year, Gerardo tried to prove to me he could change. He helped me with chores around the house. He cooked. He washed the clothes. He even encouraged me to pursue my dream of becoming a real estate agent.

In March 2001, I began taking a class that was taught by a retired Texas real estate attorney to get my real estate license. I was determined to become financially independent, in part because unresolved conflicts between Gerardo and me simmered beneath the surface of our relationship. He was still angry and resentful about my marriage to Fernie. And I was not over Fernie. Though I'd cut off contact with him, about a year later, after Gerardo had said something cruel to me, I broke down and called Fernie. I told him I needed a friend but we could only communicate by phone. Worried that Gerardo would find out, I bought a cell phone that I used just for talking and texting with Fernie and kept it hidden. Our friendship remained just that: a friendship. We never saw each other in person, and I vented to him about Gerardo, mainly. Fernie became my lifeline, as I had no one else to lean on. All I knew was that love was a powerful force that infused me with strength to carry on during those times. With Fernie's support, I slowly came to realize that Gerardo would not allow me to break free. I became terrified of his anger and physical assaults. I feared for my life.

One day, while I was showering, Gerardo found my second cell phone and went through it without my permission. He saw Fernie's phone number in my address book and our text messages, and he stormed into the bathroom, angrily ripping back the shower curtain and confronting me about it. Then he called Fernie and told him to stay away from me. Gerardo didn't believe we were just friends and went to search for him in the apartment complex where he lived in Richardson, Texas, about twenty miles away from us.

I quickly called Fernie to warn him Gerardo was looking for him. I told him Gerardo had a gun. Fernie called me later, saying, "I see your husband's truck. I see Gerardo's truck." I told him to run, but Gerardo saw Fernie at the bottom of the staircase to the apartment complex, and Fernie took off running with Gerardo chasing after him.

Just as Gerardo was reaching for his gun, Junior called him to see when he was coming home to take him to the store, because Gerardo had promised to take him to buy a video game.

The call brought Gerardo to his senses, and he left the apartment complex.

After that, I realized I had to forever sever all communication with Fernie. At this point, I knew the ugly dark side of Gerardo's constant control, anger, and jealousy, and my life, as well as Fernie's, was in danger. I called to tell Fernie this while Gerardo was at his weekend job, delivering inflatables for birthday parties, and had taken the boys with him. Fernie begged me not to give up on us, saying he'd wait for me. I told him our dream of being together could never happen, and Fernie sang a song to me. It was a Spanish tune that talked about a foreigner, a very poor man, who had fallen in love with a woman of a better social economic status. That was how he saw us. I cried and told him, "I will always love you." He told me the same. This decision broke my heart to pieces. We just never could make our way back to each other, but Fernie's love empowered me until the end of our relationship.

***

In December 2001, we decided to sell our home because Gerardo did not feel comfortable there. It reminded him too much of what had happened between Fernie and me. I also suspect that he wanted to sell because Fernie knew where we lived, and he did not like that. Alan and Junior were in middle school, and John was in high school. They were all doing so well there, and I didn't want to uproot them once again, but Gerardo ignored my pleas, and we moved into a different property, back in Mesquite, which Gerardo had purchased.

We soon realized the Mesquite school district was not like the Garland school district. I had developed a rapport with the Garland staff and could call them up if I had any questions. In Mesquite, we had to set up appointments to talk. We saw an ad for a two-story home in Garland from a young wife who wanted to sell on a lease-purchase basis. For the sake of the boys, who missed their friends, we bought this home and moved back to Garland. It didn't solve our problems, though. Far from it.

Gerardo had bought the home in Mesquite to prove that he was the sole income earner. He managed to trap me again in a position of financial dependence while stripping me of my self-esteem. When we decided to sell the home, Gerardo placed an ad in a Spanish newspaper. Rosy, a pretty young Latin girl, showed up at our doorstep telling me she was the buyer. Gerardo decided to sell the house also on a lease-purchase basis.

As we settled back into Garland in 2003, I discovered that Gerardo had been having an affair with Rosy. I discovered several notes in his paperwork and addresses to a bar and motels. Eventually I was able to prove it. I was shocked and angry. I demanded he take back the house from Rosy, as she was late on payments. After we evicted her, Gerardo found a way to help her refinance the home. He and Rosy had an affair for a year, but I didn't expose him because I didn't want to hurt our boys.

I became determined to try to rebuild my relationship with Gerardo so our boys could grow up in a loving household. I tried to show him in every way possible that I was truly sorry for leaving him. I initiated marriage counseling, and Gerardo came to two sessions. In those sessions, I expressed remorse, shame, and guilt, while Gerardo exhibited repressed anger. At me.

He still had major trust issues with me, which I could understand. I tried to talk openly with him, but he didn't believe in counseling. I know now I was living in a broken relationship, but I was broken myself. It would have taken a lot of energy and courage to leave this toxic situation, and that was energy I did not have. I was too poorly equipped to live on my own and support myself, so I stayed with him. Unconsciously or consciously, I thought I deserved Gerardo's anger—that I literally deserved punishment for having fallen in love with his half brother. And maybe I did. I was ashamed of myself, and I took full responsibility for all the pain I caused in my marriage.

I tried to assuage this guilt by overcompensating with my parenting, often giving the boys too much money or just giving them everything they wanted, whatever I could afford. Gerardo criticized me for that too. I attempted to regain Gerardo's trust by allowing him to have access to my work emails and my phone. I thought that by doing this, I would be showing him that I was willing to work extra hard on our marriage, that I was committed to my children and to my husband. Instead, it just kept me even more tightly under his control.

I took all his punishment silently and for the sake of my children. I did not want them to grow up as I had, in a broken home. What I wanted most for them was their total safety and emotional well-being. We'd bought Cody, a Pomeranian, for the boys, but Gerardo refused to allow him inside our home. We had to keep him in the garage despite the fact that it was a scorching-hot Texas summer. This broke my heart and the children's hearts as well. John would sneak him inside when Gerardo was at work, but for the most part he had to stay in the garage. I felt helpless.

At the same time, we'd entered a new phase of success in our professional—rather, in my professional—real estate career. I say "our" because Gerardo had inserted himself into that as well.

Once I began to look back at everything I'd done, for the first time, I realized I'd accomplished and gained so much on my own. The problem was that Gerardo continually stripped me of all my sense of worth, and my self-esteem would hit rock bottom during his incidents of verbal rage. I was shrinking into myself, in so much emotional pain and distress that I withdrew, allowing Gerardo to take all the credit. My sons often saw the reactive side of Gerardo's oppression and knew I was in turmoil. I was unable to protect them emotionally, and while I gave them everything I had, the truth is that I had very little. Gerardo's constant torment emptied me out.

After I took the required 270 hours of classes, I applied for my real estate license. I passed the Texas real estate exam on my first try and the national portion the following day. I remember looking at my exam sheet over and over. For the first time, aside from when I'd given birth to my children, I was proud of myself. I'd passed both tests, even though I had a sixth-grade education. It closed a door on a very painful chapter of my life. I'd been deprived of so much when Cesar had kidnapped me, not the least of which was my education, and I saw this as reclaiming part of what he'd stolen. Looking at those test results felt like looking at a college degree. I had taken steps to empower myself and created a career path.

I began working at Century 21, where I learned from the top-selling agents. Not long after that, I obtained my insurance license so I could sell many different types of insurance. Gerardo took over the front lines, speaking with and interviewing clients and showing them homes, even though he didn't have a real estate license. This was close to, but did not cross, the line of practicing real estate without a license. He took all the glory, it seemed, while I was making the real estate deals happen behind the scenes. I negotiated the contracts myself.

He became so enmeshed in establishing himself in my career that his own full-time manufacturing job suffered—and his superiors noticed. So one day in 2002, he came home and told me he'd lost his job of ten years because he had been neglecting his work while managing my real estate career. This meant we lost our health insurance. He still controlled all our finances and refused to pay for my prescriptions or therapy out of pocket. Gerardo didn't trust me, not even while I was at work. He began shadowing me and popping into my office for visits. He didn't like that I had male coworkers and closely watched how I interacted with them. If I was friendly, Gerardo accused me of being interested in these male agents. Soon enough, he began to ask that I go to the office only when I was meeting clients and only during the day, which I agreed to do. I was an independent contractor, so I had the freedom to make such a decision. Gerardo kept tabs on me, tagging along when my associates would invite me to a lunch, dinner, Saturday birthday party, or networking event. If I had evening appointments, he insisted on going with me. I had no choice but to allow Gerardo into my personal space.

Still, my career was expanding. I found it very rewarding, and I worked tirelessly, determined to send all three of my boys to college. But underneath it all, I was not happy.

In addition, John was getting more and more angry and difficult to deal with. During his junior year of high school, he had been going out a lot, partying and coming home during the wee hours of the morning. He'd even wrecked one of our cars. He and Gerardo often clashed, which created even more tension in our household.

I finally confronted him after he came home one of those late nights and told him we had to talk the next day. That's when he revealed he was struggling as a result of his sexual identity and scared to tell us that he was in a relationship with another man. It was something I'd suspected, and I was just relieved he finally felt he could tell me. I told him I loved him and there was nothing to be embarrassed about. After that, the wild partying stopped.

He got accepted to Southern Methodist University that fall. We helped with tuition, as did his father. I was proud to have instilled the value of education in my boys, for giving them what I never had myself. During his sophomore year, John finally told Charles he was gay, but his father didn't take it as well as I had. Charles was still deeply committed to his religion, which opposed any type of same-sex relationship, and he stopped paying his share of tuition. John had to drop out of SMU and started going to a local community college instead. Charles's rejection was hard for me to understand. How can you claim to be a Christian when you deny your own flesh and blood?

***

In July 2003, I decided to get bariatric surgery. Obesity ran in my family, and after I had Alan, I'd begun struggling with my weight and had ballooned up to nearly three hundred pounds. I'd tried fen-phen (an anti-obesity treatment that used two now-banned drugs) in the late '90s and lost fifty pounds, but I'd quickly gained it back. When I'd been with Fernie, I'd lost weight on my own by eating healthier and taking daily walks. But once I'd gotten back with Gerardo, I'd started gaining again.

When I was unhappy or feeling anxious, I took refuge in food. It was yet another way to try to fill that emotional void in me that had been there since childhood. We live in a society where physical appearance can determine job security, high wages, and promotions at work. I certainly felt like I was treated differently at social gatherings. Having this surgery was a last resort, but one I desperately needed. Afterward, I began to lose quite a bit of weight, which was a major victory for me.

As I honed my work skills, we switched to a smaller real estate brokerage that would give us a higher percentage of the business we brought in, and soon my career (and Gerardo's) took off. While it was exciting at first, money would soon become lord over our lives.

We began to advertise in multiple newspapers. I helped our business grow as an associate and assistant loan processor, until Gerardo and I eventually formed our own real estate branch. At that point, I became a real estate broker after taking another 180-hour course. We were making a lot of sales in real estate. With this success came the desire to upgrade to the home of our dreams. Gerardo and I had always wanted land, and we found a foreclosed home with almost 2.5 acres in Garland. We decided to apply for a mortgage. Gerardo's credit had more dings than mine, so I managed to secure what, back then, was called a stated-income loan—a loan based on your stated, not verified, income. It had been seven years since the bankruptcy, and I had hired a firm to remove all the negative credit accounts; as a result, my credit score had risen quite a bit. We found a client to take over the lease-purchase of the two-story home we'd been living in and settled into our dream home right before the summer of 2004.

Our business was doing so well that we were able to afford

nice vacations and much more. Gerardo and I had never ever experienced so much success, and the children appeared to be happy. But this success also revealed the dark side of Gerardo's machismo. Our success meant a lot of career socializing, and after I lost all that weight, I attracted male attention from peers and colleagues. Some was purely professional, and some was men flirting—and because Gerardo, of course, did not allow me to attend any social gatherings unless he was present, I settled for complacency in this role. I learned to become submissive, not by choice but rather as part of the machismo culture.

What does machismo look like? This is how I can describe it: it is the instilling of negative beliefs about how men must be aggressively masculine and how women must be submissive to them. It stems from male authority figures, such as fathers, stepfathers, and uncles, and is passed down the line to sons. It is purely about control. Machismo is the word primarily used in Latino culture, though this practice is also seen in cultures around the world.

All my husbands had machismo traits. It began with Cesar, the first monster, and then continued with each ex-husband. I'd been kept small, confined, subservient, and submissive. As a result, I was codependent, and I remained in an endless cycle of toxic relationships.

Machismo behaviors are learned from an early age, and if they are not recognized, adults who grew up in abusive households can revictimize their own children. My ability to cope was often thwarted and overwhelmed by these expectations. I became depressed. My parental authority had been stripped away by Gerardo, which limited my ability to teach my boys good living skills. My children saw me as a reactive person rather than a proactive parent. And as I myself lived in such a tightly controlled environment, my bond with my children was compromised. I became trapped in a competition with Gerardo for my sons' loyalties. They saw him as a good parent and me as the bad one for making that one mistake—marrying Gerardo's half brother.

In time, I do hope that the real Gerardo will be exposed, that they will see he is not the father they know, that he is different when it is just the two of us.

9

The Bubble Bursts

I wanted an easy fix that would take away the emotional and physical pain I was experiencing, but by doing so, I made things worse. I began taking medications without truly understanding what I was doing to myself.

A doctor first prescribed me muscle relaxants and mild anti-inflammatory medication in 2004 for the lingering pain from the back and spine injuries I'd sustained in my car accidents. When those didn't work, he began gradually introducing me to OxyContin, fentanyl patches, and tramadol, which I didn't realize were highly addictive. Nor did I realize that the body becomes resistant to opioids, which causes it to need more and more to get the same relief. I kept taking the medications because I trusted my doctor. I also began spending in secret again, racking up thousands of dollars of debt.

Somehow, I still managed to function, and by 2006 our careers were not just thriving but flourishing. We moved into our own office space in May of that year, and in July we met a colleague who was also experienced in real estate and was thriving. She introduced us to the mortgage side of the business and sponsored Gerardo so he could get a loan officer license, even though he had no knowledge of the job. I was still doing all the nitty-gritty, behind-the-scenes work on the loans and real estate deals, but Gerardo was the one getting the awards and recognition.

He was named loan officer of the year more than once. I almost wept one time because I felt like those recognitions should have been mine. Not only did I negotiate the real estate contracts and fulfill all the duties of a personal assistant, but I was also the loan processor. I was the one putting in all the effort, the sweat that went into preparing those long files. We specialized in helping lower-income families get mortgages. I went the extra mile, gathering all the documents they would need, though the families probably never knew it. They looked up to Gerardo and thought he was really someone special for helping make their loans go through. Yet I was the one putting in extra hours because Gerardo refused to hire a receptionist or loan processor. I finally broke down in tears and told him I couldn't do it all anymore, and while he agreed to hire a part-time receptionist and use a loan-processing firm, we still had to work long days. The woman we'd hired and I would still be there until 7:00 or 8:00 p.m. every day, overwhelmed and trying to get all the paperwork in, but Gerardo couldn't see the strain it caused. He had no appreciation for women or what he considered women's tasks.

The popular stated-income mortgage loans were our bread and butter. The client just had to have a good credit score and a solid job to buy a home that was two or three times their income. As a result, many people were buying homes they could not truly afford—this would eventually lead to the 2008 real estate market crash that was looming on the horizon.

We worked hard that year and the next and were bringing in $25,000 to $30,000 a month. We went on luxurious vacations to the Caribbean islands, Hawaii, Cabo San Lucas, Cancún, the Bahamas, Disney World, and Puerto Vallarta. Sometimes we took our extended families with us. I bought my family extravagant presents like designer purses, diamond jewelry, and fur coats. We were hosting family parties with mariachi bands, expensive alcohol, and catered food. We were truly living life in the fast lane, and while I enjoyed the perks, deep down, I knew I was only desperately trying to fill the void inside me with all this luxury. During this time, my constant working was partly fueled by Little Nikki's desperate plea for love and approval. My efforts gained praise from Gerardo—he was always affectionate when I was earning money. Little Nikki would retreat, feeling satisfied, but she was always just below the surface, waiting for the next criticism or violent word to strike me. I ended up on a roller coaster of emotions, confused by Gerardo's alternating charming love and cutting cruelty.

Gerardo was also increasingly controlling in all aspects of our life. At home, I could not make any decisions regarding the upkeep of our house. Gerardo did not want me to hire anyone to come to the home because the workers were usually male, and he did not want me alone in the house with another man. I would spend hours trying to obtain his permission to hire contractors to perform basic home maintenance. He did agree to have a $30,000 in-ground pool built after the boys begged him for it, but he was involved in every detail, and I had to ask permission to make each payment to the contractors.

That year, we spent the holidays traveling. After our

company's Christmas party in December 2007, we surprised Gerardo's family in Mexico with a visit to celebrate all our success. Christmas traditions in Mexico are huge. Families typically make elaborate nativity scenes, have traditional Spanish Christmas caroling, and hold dancing parties coupled with fireworks, hot cocoa, piñatas, tamales, and candy bags for the children.

We provided the food, candy, drinks, and tokens for raffle prizes, not to mention the mariachi bands. And last but not least, we also brought the customary bottles of tequila. This was almost a ritual for the locals. Having grown up without any family traditions, I loved all this. Gerardo's grandmother showered us with love, as she did many residents of the small town that she lived in. There, women were the caretakers and nurturers, and men were the providers and protectors, so Gerardo's family saw him as a hero for paying for all the Christmas expenses. Little did they know that I was making a lot of the money myself, even though I had to beg to get any of it. Gerardo would allocate me a certain amount, and I always asked for more. When he wouldn't give it to me, I would still buy what I wanted, putting the rest on credit cards.

Still, for those short years, Christmases were joyous for me. I truly felt loved and welcomed, especially by Gerardo's grandmother. Yet, despite the joy, it was still a difficult holiday for me, reminding me I'd grown up with no parental love. So I indulged in excessive eating, drinking, and shopping to drown out all the pain. I was also on the heavy painkillers, and I had begun to drink hard liquor, whiskey in particular.

After Mexico in 2007, we headed to New York City to ring in the new year at Madison Square Garden. It was a dream come true. To outsiders, we must have looked like a happy family. No one could see my pain—I hid it so very well from

the world and especially from my sons. Having grown up in
poor families with few resources, Gerardo and I were shining
examples of living the American dream.

Until we weren't.

***

Gerardo and I continued working together, though he was
still the one in charge. I wanted to expand our business and
had a ton of ideas, but I wasn't allowed to act on them. I enjoyed networking, but the fact is I could only do so much with
professional business colleagues by phone. I thought we could
possibly expand our real estate and loan brokerage into a fran-
chise, but Gerardo dismissed my suggestion and asked where
I was going to get the money to do that. I wanted to explore
getting funding from the Small Business Administration, but I
just didn't have the strength to challenge Gerardo. I was afraid
of him crushing me emotionally. I believe our real estate and
insurance business would have grown on a much larger scale
if I'd been allowed to do this, but I couldn't express how I was
feeling. So I continued to turn to unhealthy addictions like
overspending, overeating, drinking too much, and taking too
many addictive painkillers to drown the pain. Deep inside I
knew these were all just temporary fixes, but I was helpless to
stop myself.

By the summer of 2008, the writing was on the wall. All
the business in real estate and subprime mortgage loan products, which was our niche, had begun to dissolve, and banks
were withdrawing the loan products and programs that were a
huge part of our success. We'd begun to see the effects of that,
but we remained hopeful that things would change. Looking
back, I can see we should have begun building a nest egg for

retirement instead. But we did not. When I tried to bring up getting a financial adviser, Gerardo shot me down. He did not approve of spending money on such things, saying that financial advisers lived off dumb people. I supposed he was speaking about me.

I did not even have time to enjoy our new pool because I was working so much. At the end of the workday, I was too exhausted to do anything but collapse into bed. I felt so hopeless, seeing no end to the work demands. Gerardo would stonewall me every time I attempted to lighten my workload. Instead, he brought in even more new clients. There were times I'd simply lie there and cry. I was just so tired. Nothing helped fill that void inside me, that emptiness, and no unhealthy addiction could dull my underlying pain.

I had booked a family trip to Cancún that summer, and by the time it came around, we were starting to feel the loss of income. I was borrowing money just to repay other debts. My credit card debt was also increasing. I was starting to worry that the real estate market crash was going to destroy what we had built, but I couldn't stop spending. Or drinking. Or taking pills. The trip piled even more debt onto our credit cards.

Our second night at the hotel, I spent most of the time at the swim-up bar at the pool, drinking tequila shots and Buchanan's Scotch, my favorite whisky. I met a family at the bar and struck up a good conversation with the husband, who was in the real estate business in California. By 5:00 p.m., I was so drunk that when Gerardo and our sons tried to get me to leave, I wouldn't. Meanwhile, the man's wife and some other tourists were so drunk they were daring another lady to strip in plain daylight. At that point, Gerardo pulled me out of the water roughly by my arm, and the lifeguards told everyone it was time to get out of the pool. I refused to speak to Gerardo;

Junior and Alan each held one of my hands. Finally, a kind hotel employee talked to me softly and convinced me I needed to rest and recover as he escorted us to our room. It is amazing how one nice person could convince me to go up to my room whereas Gerardo couldn't with his anger and physical confrontation.

The following day, all I heard were accusations. Gerardo was mad at me for "making a fool of him." He said I had disrespected him in front of our sons and the hotel guests. I'd thought I'd just been having fun, but deep down, I knew I had a problem and felt guilty. A little compassion from Gerardo would have been so healing for me, but the environment around my husband was too toxic. I turned my anger inward, which began to affect my health.

I was in a lot of physical pain, agonizing back pain and migraine headaches that were only tamed by opioid medication. But no matter what I did, the pain came back. I kept asking my doctor for different medications to try, but none of them kept the pain away. During this time, Little Nikki was in a downward spiral. I would curl up in my bed and cry, always wanting to stay indoors in the dark. Instead of investigating why I was feeling pain or trying to get me to come out, Gerardo would tell me to stay in and "rest." This was just another way he could keep me under his control, always knowing where I was, even as he spent more and more time away from home.

After our trip, our real estate and loan business began to dwindle away. Still, we remained hopeful that something would turn around. We continued to work hard—and I continued to spend. Our boys had the latest smartphones. We all wore designer clothes, and I carried designer purses. Gerardo and I had adopted the mentality that material possessions were worth working for, even to the point of burnout. We had placed the accumulation of money and possessions on a pedestal, making it the keeper of our worth and happiness.

***

As summer turned to fall, our clients were calling, worried about what they were hearing on the news about the housing crisis and interest rates rising. Our clients had adjustable-rate mortgage loans, which meant their interest rates fluctuated. On September 29, 2008, the Dow Jones fell 777 points in one day, the biggest one-day drop at that point in its history.

The drop triggered by the collapse of the housing bubble led to mortgage delinquencies and foreclosures. Lehman Brothers, a global financial services firm, declared bankruptcy, facing huge, unprecedented losses due to the continuing subprime mortgage crisis. The bigger banks—J.P. Morgan and others such as Bank of America—were rescued by a government bailout plan, but smaller ones like Wachovia Corporation fell victim to the subprime mortgage mess. Meanwhile, Washington Mutual was sold to J.P. Morgan, and with this came the downfall of other major banks. Some survived. Some did not. And we were caught up in it. All I could think about was our clients. We had never imagined such chaos.

By December 2008, I was still in denial, still secretly racking up credit card debt. Most of our clients were eventually offered affordable refinances by the bailout plan, which allowed them to salvage their homes by reducing their interest rates. Subconsciously I must have known what was coming, because my depression and anxiety had begun to take a real toll on my mental well-being. I felt, deep down, that the foundation we had built, which had been based on acquisitions instead of values, would not be enough to sustain us for what was to come.

Slowly, one by one, I began to stop making even the minimum payments on my credit cards. I changed my phone number to stop creditors from calling me. That Christmas was worse than I could have imagined, especially since our whole world and worth revolved around owning material possessions. I began to develop another panic disorder. My hands always felt sweaty, and I had breathing problems, a racing heart. The worst part was that I had absolutely no control over these feelings. My thinking became foggy. I felt drained. I had no energy, and I avoided going out, content to stay home curled up in bed. It was like a slow death. Fear was gripping me, and I needed medical help.

Our 2007 Chevy truck got repossessed after we stopped making the payments in order to afford basics like food, bills, and house payments. The mortgage became a priority, and I applied for government assistance for food. Gerardo took odd jobs, like working for a moving service; he had surrendered his loan officer license and I surrendered my real estate broker license because we couldn't afford the fees to keep them active. We just let them expire. The life we had built with all that hard work and sacrifice had come crashing down, and by early 2009, we were barely getting by.

What was even worse was that we had to stop helping our sons pay for college. Junior managed with student loans and by taking on odd jobs. Alan wanted to go to the University of Texas at Dallas with hopes of obtaining a degree in computer engineering and had applied for student financial aid. John continued his biology classes at a local community college. I vowed to push myself to ensure my sons could continue their educations. I stayed in my room and began to sell my designer purses, clothes, and shoes on eBay. Then, I started buying wholesale products from China and reselling them at a higher price, doing everything in my power to bring in some income and ensure my sons could continue pursuing their dreams.

In January 2009, Daddy Lou and my mom stopped by on my birthday. I was in bed. The depression was by now beginning to interfere with my daily activities, but just seeing Daddy Lou cheered me up. He'd bought me a pair of cute socks with Chihuahuas on them because he knew that I liked them. Mom brought a ceramic doll. I was starting to see that she did care for me in her own way. I had to remember that Mom herself was still a little girl, that she too was emotionally stunted.

In March 2009, Gerardo began taking a full-time course to become a commercial truck driver, with the help of Robert, who had been a truck driver for years. It is not an easy profession. Truck drivers typically work long hours and basically live and sleep in their eighteen-wheeler rigs, whether they own or rent them. Their lives are largely solitary because they spend the majority of the day driving, and they struggle with constant pressures of hauling goods like food and other essentials. They spend very little time at home. Gerardo had financed a used eighteen-wheeler rig, so he and Robert were hauling sand and gravel to new construction sites throughout the nation's largest states.

By the fall of 2009, we were caught up on our mortgage payments, but my codependence on my sons and my husband was so strong that Gerardo's absence only assisted in sending me into that deep hole of severe depression. I was taking OxyContin and Valium, but I was also drinking too much. The combination almost became lethal.

One Friday, I called Gerardo and told him I was lying on the floor and could not stand up. I had overdosed. Gerardo asked that I stay on the line until he could reach one of our boys. Alan had arrived home from college—as if heaven-sent—and made his way to check up on me. He'd taken first aid classes in high school, so he knew what to do. He checked my pulse, then gently slapped me on the face to rouse me. After I was alert, he stood me up, where he performed a Heimlich-like maneuver to get me to throw up, which I did. Over and over again. He wanted to call an ambulance, but I told him not to. I knew Gerardo would be angry.

Gerardo had to drop his delivery to come home. When he arrived, instead of taking me to the hospital, he told me I had to deal with my alcoholism, then went to the store to get me a Mexican mineral water that is supposed to be good for hangovers.

It was clear I was on my own.

**

We began searching for another way for Gerardo to make a living that would enable him to stay closer to home, mostly so he could care for me. I still had a phobia of driving after so many accidents, and I found myself totally dependent on him to take me to all my doctor appointments. He took on household chores and some cooking. I knew that his main objective was to help me, but it also kept me isolated. He was my entire support system.

Around this time, I was diagnosed with "severe and chronic dissociative identity disorder, not otherwise specified," which had previously been known as multiple personality disorder. In the same way the body can wall off an abscess or foreign substance to protect the rest of the body, the brain can disassociate from trauma. The brain will work to avoid the painful memories, sometimes splitting into two or more personalities, each with no memory of what the other has experienced.

Little Nikki was beginning to understand that if she could please Gerardo, he would shower her with love and praise. So all her energy went toward making him happy. Gerardo began asking for anal sex more often, and Little Nikki would give in, too scared and shy to fend him off despite the fact that it hurt and wasn't what I wanted. He would give me alcohol so that it would be less painful, which felt off, given that he'd just told me I needed to deal with my alcoholism. Giving him his way meant that I could get him to caress me and make me feel loved, though, and he knew that was what I wanted. Little Nikki suffered in silence.

Gerardo also began making more of an effort to do things with me and get me out of the house, so we began going to dance halls again occasionally. He encouraged me to drink when we went. Gerardo was very possessive at the dance halls; there were always more single men than single women, and he would get very jealous when we were there. One evening, we stayed till closing. After the band announced that the bar would close in fifteen minutes, I glanced at a couple we'd seen arguing earlier that night and saw them stand up and make their way outside. There were always various food vendors— tacos, hot dogs, and so on—and it was customary for people to gather and eat outside after the dances were over.

We joined the milling crowd outside, but something inside me felt wrong. I saw the young couple eating at the hot dog stand, and I asked Gerardo to buy me a taco. As we were ordering, an old Ford truck with a camper came to a screeching halt outside the dance hall. Suddenly, the woman of the young couple yelled, "No, no, don't kill me!" Shots rang out.

There was a gunman in the back part of the camper, and he had fired multiple shots at the young couple before the truck sped off. People were running and yelling, but the young lady lay still on the ground, looking lifeless. She was wearing white jeans, and I can remember the blood gushing from her. Her boyfriend had been shot twice in his arm but appeared to be holding up, so I asked him why someone would do such a thing to her. He told me her ex-husband was the shooter. Soon after that, ambulances and police cars began to fill up the dusty gravel parking lot.

I couldn't believe her ex-husband had shot this couple just because she had rejected him. At the same time, I could. This man, in his anger, must have felt fully justified in doing it; at some dance halls, for a man to show interest in another man's woman is to gamble with his life.

There are many stories and songs in the Latino culture about two *machista* men fighting for a woman. In this sense, women are more like trophies, and the men are equated with knights. But once conquered, she matters little. She's just a shiny object that proves the man's dominance. And as a result of the "conquer" mentality, the younger generation often looks up to machista men as an example to follow. Machista men at Latin dance halls exemplify these attitudes, as they prioritize "winning" women as opposed to respecting and seeing them as equals.

I never found out if the young lady survived or not, though I've never forgotten her.

Gerardo's response was simply "That's what happens when a man is not respected." I felt threatened by his words, and a wave of anxiety came over me. I recalled all the blatant machismo he'd often displayed and the aggression and possessiveness he'd showed toward me. I was chilled by the incident; that young woman so easily could have been me.

***

Even with the money troubles and mental health issues, we were still a family, albeit a dysfunctional one.

Christmas 2010 was an extraordinary time. The boys had picked out the perfect gift for me: a six-week-old pure-bred Chihuahua. Cody, our Pomeranian, had tragically died in November 2006, just before Thanksgiving, and I had never been able to grieve for him. We'd been without a dog ever since. I named my little fur baby Rocky, after Rocky Road, my favorite ice cream. He cared for me during some very lonely times, and we formed a loving bond like none I'd ever had.

When Gerardo traveled, Alan would shuttle me around to doctor appointments, the grocery store, and the pharmacy to pick up and drop off prescriptions. He was still living at home while attending the University of Texas at Dallas and was now commuting back and forth in the used truck Gerardo had bought him.

I also continued to rack up a lot of debt, which Gerardo found out about after I was served with a judgment when I stopped paying my American Express bill. I owed them $28,000 for just three months of spending. And that was only one of the many credit cards I had. Gerardo became enraged and screamed at me. In February 2011, we were forced to file another Chapter 13 bankruptcy to restructure our $200,000 in debt and come up with a repayment plan. We were being hounded by creditors because we couldn't afford to make the payments. Our first bankruptcy was purely based on my un-healthy credit card spending. The bulk of it was this time, as well, but Gerardo had also purchased a $53,000 truck that we couldn't afford.

I knew it was a problem, but I shopped to relieve my anxiety and depression. It comforted and soothed me and made me feel like I fit in. It helped me feel empowered and was the only time I felt I had some control over my life. Between the spending, being overprescribed opioids, and drinking too much because of Gerardo's absences, I began to slowly wither away. Rocky was my sole source of comfort.

Then one day Gerardo came and told me that I really had to deal with my drinking, that it was an embarrassment to our boys. He asked, "Do you want them to grow up remembering you as a drunk?" That was soul crushing to hear. I was so ashamed. My sons were watching their mom wither away from depression, anxiety, substance abuse, and codependence. I begged for his forgiveness and vowed to quit. In the end, though, he wasn't telling me anything I didn't already know about myself.

Somehow, I always ended up feeling responsible for everything I did, even if it wasn't my fault. Gerardo had this way of making me feel lower than a bug, and I'd apologize to him no matter the situation. Today, I realize that being raised in an unloving home with unsupportive parents meant I was primed to always feel that everything was my fault. While I wasn't able to have that level of self-awareness back then, I did know that I needed to stop drinking, both for my boys and for myself.

Not long after that, we went to see Daddy Lou, who was in the hospital, dying of cirrhosis of the liver. He knew how much I'd been drinking in recent years and tearfully asked me to promise him I'd stop so I didn't end up like him. I knew he only wanted the best for me, so I told him I would. Daddy Lou died two weeks later, on February 11, 2011.

I had been mixing alcohol with painkillers for some time. It had gone from beer to wine to hard liquor. The loneliness, the sadness, the depression, and the hopelessness had led me to self-medicate with alcohol, which in turn had become an addiction. I knew quitting drinking wouldn't be easy, and the withdrawal symptoms were as bad as I had feared they would be. But that year, I stopped drinking alcohol, though it would still be some time before I was able to get off the opioids.

Once I became sober, I tackled another unhealthy addiction I had struggled with for years: smoking, which had always been my fix. I started by switching from smoking regular menthol cigarettes to vaping an electronic cigarette. The first week was horrible. I battled anxiety and moodiness and had trouble concentrating. As all the aforementioned symptoms were at their peak, it took me a good two weeks until I made it through with e-cigs. But I did it and was smoke-free within three months.

The loss of Daddy Lou was the tipping point for me. I so valued the love and care he'd always given me. I'd felt like a real daughter, truly loved in his arms. Seeing him lose the struggle with his own dependence issues was a wake-up call. The trauma of my past didn't have to define my future, and I certainly didn't want it to define the futures of my sons. Getting sober and over my addictions made me feel powerful. Finally, here was a true way to gain control over myself—my body and my life. I felt I was getting back on track and could become the person I wanted to be, someone who was a role model and good provider for my children.

10

Fostering My Heart

Around the spring of 2011, I was on the internet and came across an ad a local church had placed to recruit foster parents on behalf of the Texas Department of Family and Protective Services. I felt for those children who had no one to love them; I'd once been one of them. I was also feeling guilty about my overspending, and I wanted to give back in some way. These children needed love, and I intimately understood where they were coming from. Gerardo's words about the effect my drinking had on our children still rang in my ears. Maybe, in some way, it would make up for the mistakes I'd made with them. I set up an appointment, and Gerardo dropped me off that Saturday.

While at this meeting, I met a very nice lady by the name of Hazel, and we quickly bonded. She was an older woman and a mother herself, which I was always drawn to, given my past.

I opened up to her about that. She was sympathetic and just listened, without judging me. I came out of that meeting determined to save my marriage and take this new idea of becoming a foster parent very seriously. Despite the issues we had as a couple, Gerardo was a hard worker and a good provider. *We would be perfect foster parents,* I thought.

Our finances were slowly getting into better shape. We were not out of the woods yet, but we were able to stay afloat, to pay our bills and meet our basic needs. I had been sober since my promise to Daddy Lou and was determined to stay that way. It wouldn't be easy, but I knew I needed to do it for myself, our children, and the foster children we were hoping to bring into our home.

We applied to our local child protective services agency to become foster parents. The licensing process included a background check, classes, home studies, and ensuring our home passed the tough licensing standards. We began taking our classes, which gave us the chance to interact with other foster parents. I was excited and began to embrace this new journey of ours. We flew through the forty hours of shadowing a foster family in their home, which taught us the basics. By September 2011, we were officially licensed foster parents. We were approved to have up to six children in our home, since we had plenty of bedrooms for them.

Then came the hard part: picking the children we would care for. The agency sent us packets of detailed information on each child, from the time they'd entered foster care until the present. Reading through the case histories of their biological families, we couldn't help but feel immense compassion for the difficult circumstances they had faced, including instances of abuse, neglect, and the challenges arising from substance abuse. Many of these children had experienced such hardships from a very young age, which resonated deeply with my own experiences.

These files also included the child's gender and ethnicity, whether they had any siblings, and their medical needs, if any. We were told to be very careful with the administration of any medication they'd been prescribed and to keep the medications under lock and key at all times. The files also revealed any "placement disruptions" a child had had, which is what it's called when a foster parent can no longer care for a child because their behavior is disruptive to the other children in their home.

I was steadily reading through as many files as I could, trying to pick the perfect fit for foster children in our home. There were so many devastated children that had been left behind or torn from their families—how could I choose? There was just such a strong need for foster parents that I decided to take in some hard cases, severely traumatized children. These children were the forgotten ones, in many ways. I struggled with guilt over the fact that we could only have six children at a time, but it was all that we were approved for, and, quite honestly, all that we could handle.

Deciding who to bring into our home was difficult, but caring for them once they arrived was the toughest task I would ever have, though it was one I came to love.

And I had so much love to give. So did Gerardo, in his own way. I saw that he was protective of and cared for our foster children. Our first two arrived around 10:00 p.m. in September 2011. Their father had been arrested for domestic abuse, so child protective services (CPS) had to remove them and find an emergency placement for them, which was us.

They were siblings, little boys—one was two, and the other was a baby. They were scared, and the two-year-old wouldn't stop crying for his mommy. My heart went out to them. The two-year-old had arrived with no diapers on, so off went Gerardo to the twenty-four-hour Walmart to buy diapers.

Next came three more siblings. I quickly became attached, especially to the younger ones. The youngest was two years old. The older sibling said he just wanted to sleep. Lord knows what the small children had witnessed just hours before they'd arrived in our home.

For the children, the transition from their birth families into foster care was often incredibly challenging. The children—of all ages—had to deal with a new environment away from their families and full of different rules and expectations. Even in cases when a foster home was more stable than the place they came from, it was still a shock to their system. We enlisted the assistance of therapists to support the children's emotional and behavioral needs. The therapists helped us with individualized treatment plans aimed at teaching the children healthy coping skills. Additionally, we worked with teachers and counselors to create individualized education plans (IEP) to support their academic progress.

A foster parent's responsibility is to assist in helping them manage their emotions. This includes investing emotionally in each child, forming a healthy foster parent bond. No two foster children are the same. They are all unique. Navigating house rules, routines, and schedules, transporting them to and from school, activities, and medical visits—we quickly learned that foster parenting would take a lot of time and effort on our part, which we gladly gave.

It was well worth it, especially when the children bonded

with us, total strangers. I truly loved all the children that came through our home, though I came to learn foster parenting is not for the faint of heart.

***

The first few days or months of a foster child placement can be hard. These children often came to us neglected and needed routine, stability, and consistency. When a foster family places a thirty-day notice to a caseworker requesting placement termination, children are yanked out of their routines and have to adjust to new schools with new foster parents and new after-school activities. They have to learn our rules and boundaries, get accustomed to our schedules, and sometimes be taught basic living skills like brushing their teeth and wearing clean clothes. These children need stability so badly that even sending them off to the summer camps recommended by the foster agencies to help them develop social skills can be a disruptive trigger, leading them into a downward spiral and causing an explosion. As a result, we faced a lot of new challenges.

Each time they'd tearfully tell me about their own trauma, it would strike a chord with me, and I would give them the recognition and appreciation they craved. I don't think I can fully describe the joys and sorrows of seeing some of them leave. Some of the foster children left when their placements ended, which meant some would return home. And some would leave the foster system at age eighteen.

In early 2012, we decided to take in teenagers as well. We knew these were the hardest to parent, that many had spent years in the system. Some had placement disruptions in their case history, which creates a whole other level of trauma for the children as they are rejected yet again. And the teens were a challenge. They yelled, they cursed, and they were often aggressive with the other foster children. Some of them also had an extremely low tolerance for frustration in day-to-day life experiences. There were incidents where the children turned aggressive on one another; they had meltdowns, and we ended up being peacemakers, breaking up fights among them. I learned they often reenacted violence because either they had seen it or it had been inflicted upon them.

And then there were the children who were kicked out of school or summer camps for fighting and attacking other children. This, as one counselor explained, was likely due to the child's sensory overload, which triggered their fight-or-flight response. Each child came with their own unique history, traumas, and special needs. And there were always caseworker visits to our home that needed to be arranged. It is essential to have a good support system while being a foster parent, which was something I did not have. It was emotionally draining and began to take its toll on both Gerardo and me, but especially on me. It brought on symptoms that reflected back my own traumas—traumas I had not processed or dealt with yet. Little Nikki began to resurface more and more as I dealt with other aspects of fostering, such as the intense amount of paperwork that the caseworkers demanded, detailing everything about each child. Gerardo would point out my every weakness, telling me I wasn't a good mom or role model. I began feeling like my inner scared little girl all the time, so afraid to make a single misstep. I experienced symptoms of exhaustion that I could not shake off. I rapidly lost thirty-nine pounds; my anxiety was at an all-time high. Foster parenting can produce burnout, which Gerardo and I were both starting to feel.

We saw so much. There were days the children would erupt in anger, especially the teen boys, and they would hit each other, and there was little we could do but call the police or take them to inpatient twenty-four-hour psychiatric hospitals. Other times we were able to use a process called de-escalation, techniques we learned in foster parent training about how to defuse a potentially volatile situation.

It's not like taking care of one's biological children. These children often come from challenging backgrounds and may have endured abandonment, abuse, and neglect, leaving them with deep emotional scars. It's important to recognize that they may harbor feelings of blame towards their caregivers for the separation from their birth families. The change of family environment may make it difficult for them to trust and form attachments. While love and stability are what they often need and yearn for (just like I did when I was a child), foster children might exhibit defensive behaviors and distance themselves as a result of their fear and past trauma. The idea of abandonment can be particularly distressing to them, and even everyday activities like attending pre-K or grade school can trigger separation anxiety, especially in younger children.

Of the more than fifty placements of foster children we had, we bonded the most with our first two placements, the two-year-old boy and his baby brother. We had hopes of perhaps adopting them, and it was bittersweet when they left us to reunite with another foster family that had adopted their two older siblings. There was also a twelve-year-old boy that we bonded with, and when we began to see him excel in middle school, it was so exciting, one of the proudest moments of my time fostering. To know that we helped him with tools for his future means everything.

As the year 2014 approached, Gerardo and I were drifting apart. We didn't have much time to do the real estate work we both enjoyed, and the foster parent routines had begun to weigh heavily on our shoulders. I often felt guilty for not being able to help the children with their issues. I could not just tell them, *We're just trying to help you while your parents get back on their feet, and we are trying to reunite you with your family.* I felt the children's emotional pain from the disruption of and separation from their families. I battled extreme guilt; one group of three teenage sisters were in so much pain from missing their biological mom—a hole I could never fill for them. Yet I too was helpless; they were in the foster care system under a court order to be in our home. How do you explain that to a child?

While speaking to a therapist for the children, I learned I was experiencing secondary trauma. A foster parent's job is to work twenty-four hours a day, seven days a week with traumatized children. I listened to their stories and literally felt their pain. Empathy is a very important part of foster parenting. Unfortunately for me—as for many other foster parents—I had become so empathetic that I began to disregard and neglect my own needs. I was internalizing the trauma of our foster children. Secondary trauma is cumulative, as is listening to the children's traumatic histories and life stories over and over again. We all have different coping mechanisms, and I was poorly equipped in this area. While I was still able to be strong for them, I failed to recognize I was living in distress.

To any foster parent reading this, my advice is that when you begin to feel yourself emotionally or physically burned out, it is time to step back and evaluate yourself and the situations that provoke this anxiety. If these secondary trauma symptoms become hard to cope with and last for more than a few weeks, you need to practice self-care or take a break from fostering. Consider seeing a therapist who specializes in trauma work. Remember, our capacity to help children who have suffered depends on our own ability to practice self-care, physically, emotionally, spiritually, and socially. This will ensure we can be there for the children when they need us.

By late 2013, we began to implement an exit plan to terminate our foster parent license. It was just taking too great a toll on me emotionally. I was hurting deeply not only from secondary trauma but because I had wanted to adopt Jesse, a fourteen-year-old boy who'd come in and stolen my heart shortly after the first set of three siblings. He had mild traumatic brain injuries from shaken baby syndrome. I begged Gerardo to allow me to keep Jesse. He refused. He said Jesse had so many doctor visits and special needs that we simply could not care for him. There was also another child who'd wanted us to adopt him—Adam. He was extremely intelligent, and I encouraged him to attend college. We had bonded so well that afterward he ran away multiple times to be with us. When those two boys left our home, it permanently broke my heart. We officially ended our foster parenting journey and concluded our last foster child placement in October 2014.

I wish I'd been able to do more for these children, but in the end, I know I did my best to create a different world for them, at least for the short time they were in our lives. Being able to give back this way did heal a piece of me, as I knew that the children had at least experienced unconditional love while we cared for them, something that I had constantly sought at their age. If we set them on a better path for the future, then I know the world is a little brighter, and I'm so grateful for my part in that.

11

High Winds

As we were transitioning out of being foster parents, we pondered what to do. Both Gerardo and I missed the real estate business. It was something we excelled at, but we faced some hurdles trying to get back into it. I found out I had to retake some new continuing education classes to validate my new salesperson real estate license. So I began to study, and Gerardo began to study as well. We had applied for our licenses, but we still needed to activate them and take the test again. In the meantime, he continued taking local trucking jobs, because in Texas, you cannot practice real estate without a license.

We began to reenter the real estate market by calling old prospects and things like that. Now the gears were set in motion. I made an appointment to take my Texas real estate exams. I passed the first part with flying colors, and the second part I failed by just a few points. I immediately scheduled a retake within two days, and that time I passed. Having previously been a licensed Texas real estate broker and having put in over nine hundred hours earlier in my career meant nothing could stop me from achieving my dream.

Not satisfied with just the real estate license, I continued to push toward new goals and prepared to take my third exam in insurance. I had my Texas managing general agent license, but I needed to go for the Texas property and casualty insurance license, also known as the P&C license. In March 2015, I aced my exam and activated my Texas P&C license. This was a huge success. Gerardo managed to pass his Texas real estate exam after the third try.

It was great to have these successes in our professional lives, because our relationship with Alan had been taking a very dark turn, in a way that we unfortunately are still trying to deal with today.

Alan was always a talented, bright young man, but in 2012, he decided to take a break from school and pursue his passion: working on electronics and computers. I was crushed. We'd worked so hard to make sure our sons could go to college, and he was just a few credits shy of his degree. But there was nothing I could do, and he promised me he'd eventually go back.

Alan began working at a local electronics store, and in the summer of 2014, went to work for a larger one, where he met Amanda and they began dating. We didn't even know Alan had a girlfriend until one weekend evening in September 2014 when he blurted out that he wanted us to meet someone, then left and came back into the house with Amanda. It took us by complete surprise, though Gerardo admitted he had seen Amanda sneaking into Alan's room, which was in the detached garage that had been converted into a large master bedroom with a living room.

I welcomed her in a loving, courteous manner, offering

her something to drink and some banana nut bread I'd just made. We still had foster children at the time, and she told me she had a family member in foster care. I have to admit I was sad when Alan introduced me to her. I had such a strong bond with my sons, and I didn't want to lose that. Alan must have sensed what I was feeling, because he hugged me and told me he loved me. Amanda rolled her eyes and pulled his hand away from me. I could see the rage in her eyes every time he hugged me.

Alan had been promoted into the computer-repair department, and Amanda convinced him he didn't need to go back to get his degree because he could obtain a higher position at the store without needing one. She began to control Alan, and I knew this was the beginning of pure evil and disruption. What girlfriend would dissuade her boyfriend from graduating from college? It was evident Alan was in love, but his relationship with her would end up causing a rift in ours.

For the next few weeks, Amanda came to our home on workdays to wait for Alan so they could carpool to their jobs at the electronics store. One day we pulled up in the driveway with the minivan full of our foster children, and we tried to introduce Amanda to them. I asked her if she could say hello, and she rudely said, "I don't have time for this."

I told Alan we could not have any visitors that were not on our CPS home study, but Amanda refused to fill out the paperwork. In fact, she took it personally and used this as an excuse to say, "It looks like your mom has a problem with me being here." This was not true at all. I was simply making a statement that we had to follow procedure for our foster children. We ended up terminating our foster parenting license not long after that, so while it became a nonissue, it was a sign of things to come.

Our challenges with Amanda got worse. She had an authoritarian manner when she tried to control Alan. I began to suspect that her behavior was something Alan found familiar, as it was similar to what he'd witnessed in Gerardo's controlling behavior. This made me so sad. Amanda became difficult to manage, her terrible temper revving up especially when she drank. One night Alan left her at a nightclub because of her drinking behaviors, and she followed him home and forced her way onto our gated property by prying open the security gate.

Little by little she began sneaking into our home to sleep with Alan. Then Alan started bringing her home after work so they could hang out in his room. After that, he'd drive her to her mother's home in Carrollton, Texas, which was about a fifteen-minute drive. He was not much of a long-distance driver, and all that traveling back and forth was making him anxious.

One night in July 2015, Amanda called Gerardo at 2:00 or 3:00 a.m. to tell him that they'd been driving and had had to pull over on the highway because Alan was distraught and disoriented, having a full-blown panic attack. I asked Gerardo if I could speak with Alan. My kind, gentle mother's voice seemed to calm his anxiety.

After the second time this happened, I asked him if he wanted Amanda to stay at our home until they could find their own place to live. He was so relieved at first, but it ended up making things worse. She would bring strangers to our home and would arrive drunk herself. I also heard the way she spoke to my son: her condescending tone, her filthy language. When I expressed my concerns about all this to Gerardo, he dismissed them, saying he preferred to have his sons living at home, and if I kept up my criticism of her, I'd be one of those mothers whose daughters-in-law don't visit. So I kept quiet and suffered, forced to watch helplessly while she treated my son with anger and hatred.

Based on my experience with generational patterns, it seemed to me as if Amanda had been raised with some kind of trauma surrounding parental authority, which meant that we had to deal with someone who had a generational pattern of anger. Sadly, I think I was her target because I was attempting to set limits. Amanda expressed no empathy and hurt me to the very core. With me, she was cold and cruel.

By the second week of December 2015, Alan knew the friction and tension were causing major distress for me, exacerbating my depression and anxiety. I was getting severe migraines, stomachaches, and heart palpitations. The situation was so tense I finally asked them to find another place to live, after which Alan announced he and Amanda were moving to a relative's rental home.

Christmas that year was lonely, with only our youngest son, Junior, home from college for Christmas break. Our house felt cold and empty.

We had no idea how much worse it was about to get.

***

On the evening of December 26, 2015, a series of deadly storms with winds gusting up to 180 miles per hour swept through our town, spawning twelve different EF4 tornadoes and leaving a trail of devastated families in its wake.

The day had been unnaturally hot and humid, even by Texas standards. Something about it felt odd, off—even native Texans were talking about it. Gerardo and Junior were watching the news in the living room that night and saw the tornado warnings, but we'd lived in Tornado Alley for years and had grown almost immune to these alerts. I was in our bedroom with Rocky, reading a book about anxiety, when I heard Junior screaming, "Mom, Dad, let's get in the closet!" He'd seen the tornado coming, that black funnel cloud destroying everything in its wake.

I went into panic mode. "What's the matter, Junior?" I screamed as I ran toward him and he to me. Rocky jumped out of my arms, but there was no time to go after him.

"Get in the bathroom!" I yelled. "That's the safest place."

Our living area had large windows, and I knew it wasn't safe to be in there. Junior and I met in the hallway. I grabbed his left wrist and yelled again, "Get down to the bathroom." Junior was crying; I was scared out of my mind. I could hear the tornado moving closer; the roar of what sounded like a train filled our home. I could hear the rumble of debris hitting the house, and I just knew it was going to come down and crush us.

I didn't know where Gerardo was, but when Junior and I got to the bathroom, I yelled, "Go to the floor! Go to the floor!" We both did, and I hugged him tight and placed my head on top of his to protect him as much as I could. My only thought was to save my son. I started praying, begging God to take me and spare him. I heard things slamming into our home. It felt as if our roof had been uprooted and lifted off, and then as if it had set itself back. I thought I was going to die. All I could think to do was thank the Lord for giving me a chance at motherhood. That had been the biggest gift of my life.

I don't remember how long we lay there, holding on tight to each other, before it was over. We were frozen. Neither of us wanted to move. We stayed in the bathroom, praying and holding hands. We'd gone to Junior's bathroom because it was closer than Gerardo's and mine—a decision that ended up saving our lives. The tornado hit the right side of our home, spewing debris into our bedroom, where I'd been quietly reading just moments before. The debris hit the decking and blew away our carport. Miraculously, the part of the house where Junior and I had hidden was untouched.

Gerardo had fled to the kitchen with Rocky in his arms and squatted down to shield him. They both survived, even though the roof had caved in above them. He said he'd seen parts of his tools just blow up into the air, and to this day we don't know where they ended up.

The tornado was so strong that it picked up cars on the freeway and tossed them around. There were some fatalities—one was a mother of five children. It was so sad.

Police officers, firefighters, retired police, veterans, and volunteers went door to door in the affected areas, checking for unsafe living conditions and victims and tagging and marking structures. The firefighters spoke over the car sirens, telling us, "If you are safe and alive, stay indoors until it is safe to leave your home."

But all I could think about were our elderly neighbors. Our lives had been blessed and spared, but I thought, *What about the others?* I stepped outside our home again and was paralyzed by the horrific devastation all around us. Our neighbor, Ernie, was ninety-two, and he lived by himself. I tried to get over to his house, but an officer told me that help was on the way and to go home.

I asked Gerardo to see if he could get to Ernie while paramedics made it through the debris and the downed trees. He replied that our other neighbor was with him and said, "I can't help him." Back then, I saw nothing wrong with his reaction because I was used to his lack of empathy. The psychological violence that Gerardo had subjected me to had eaten away at the core of my being. It had stolen my self-esteem, every ounce of it. I panicked every time he spoke in that overbearing tone of voice. I would express this to him, and he would always just say, "This is how I talk."

Another neighbor had managed to evade the police and get to Ernie. He was in his wheelchair, bleeding from his head, in the midst of the wreckage of his home; the only things left were the pillars. That was one of the saddest things I've seen in my life. His house was totally destroyed. I don't know how Ernie survived. He went to a nursing home after that, and we later found out he died shortly after, though not from his injuries. I think it was from a broken heart. He'd lived in that home with his wife, and he couldn't rebuild because he didn't have insurance. I think, after the tornado, he was hit with depression. He'd lost everything.

I stood outside trying to assess the damage to our home and property. Thankfully, we all survived, but the tornado took half our house and most of our belongings. The pillars had been uprooted and were just lying on the ground. Our brick-and-iron fence had blown away. The church next door was completely gone. We were grateful to be alive but worried sick because our insurance would only cover a fraction of our losses.

It's not uncommon for heavy downpours to occur after a tornado, and that's exactly what happened. I remember standing in the middle of our driveway, sobbing, as the rain poured down into our home, destroying what the tornado hadn't already taken. I felt helpless. Everything we had worked for, everything we had sacrificed for, was being destroyed. I'd already had to overcome so much throughout my life, and now this too?

I looked up at the sky and silently raged at God. *You took everything from me, Lord. Why, why did you take my home too?* I just didn't believe he existed anymore. *Where are you? You're not real,* I thought. Just then, out of the corner of my eye, I saw a pickup truck with four or five men in it turn into our driveway.

"Can we help you?" they wanted to know. "Is there anything we can do?"

It was as if God had heard me asking those questions and these Samaritans were his answer. I just knew these contractors were heaven-sent. Gerardo, of course, questioned their good intentions, and he told me to tell them that we had no money to pay them. I told the contractor, "Thank you, but my husband says that we do not have any money to pay you." The contractor said, "No, ma'am. Do not worry. We will help you. No strings attached." I asked Gerardo if it was okay that they help us, and this time he agreed. Looking back, I do not see why I had to ask permission for the contractors to assist; it was my home. My name was the only one on the deed, at least at that time.

I told them we needed help tarping our home so the rain wouldn't destroy what little we had left, and they quickly got to work. They came in, and they started cutting the wood they had in their truck. They sealed with tarps the parts of the roof that had been blown off, cut the decking and filled it in temporarily where the water was coming in. Gerardo was scheduled to have hernia surgery in a few weeks, so he couldn't do much himself. I don't know what we would have done without them.

After they finished, they asked us if we needed something to eat. We took some water from them. We all held hands and prayed. I remember the oldest man said, "Lord, use these vessels for your glory."

It was the first of many ways those in the community opened their arms to us, an outpouring of love and support that I had never experienced before, certainly not in my own love-starved childhood. And these were strangers. The way they rallied around us didn't just restore my faith in humanity; it *gave* me a faith in humanity I'd never had before. I recall just saying, "Thank you, God. I really did not mean what I said, and you know my heart ever so well."

Later that evening, Junior decided to take Rocky and head back to his apartment in Denton, Texas, close to the university he was attending. I was still recovering from the depression and anxiety, but after he told me they made it there safely, my heart seemed to calm down.

There were still police officers all around our home, firefighters clearing and making a way for people to leave. I will never forget that night. It was the scariest night of my life. The authorities had to take precautions because of the downed power lines, the flash floods, and all the rain that followed the tornado, so there was a curfew, meaning we couldn't leave our house. We survived a dark night without power, confined to one bedroom and bathroom. Once we were able to secure a hotel room, we went back and forth to pack clothing.

We all came together, people from different parts of the area. We were placed on the Salvation Army list to see if we qualified for emergency disaster repair funds for building materials to fix our home. The next day we went to Central Park in Garland. A lot of churches, the Red Cross and the Salvation Army, and hundreds of other families were there. I saw devastation in their faces. Some had lost their whole home, some had lost parts of their home, some had had rental homes. There, we all seemed to come together. Churches from every denomination offered counseling for the brokenhearted, for the oppressed and crushed in spirit.

A Salvation Army counselor, an elderly man who must have been able to see how much distress I was in, handed me a brand-new plush Mickey Mouse toy, similar to one my sons had had growing up that had been destroyed in the tornado. I had never seen such generosity. It was like God was telling me, "You lost everything, but I'm going to return everything that you lost." The man started a conversation while we were waiting in line to speak to the Salvation Army caseworkers. I poured my heart out to this generous elderly man, and he listened to the pain and heartache that had been bottled up during my life. I guess I was just ready to release it. I still have that Mickey Mouse.

I saw many people crying that day. So many needed so much. We were given gift cards for food and vouchers for hotels and placed on a referral list for help rebuilding our home. That's where we were able to receive help for the parts that were underinsured. We were short by about $150,000, so three churches stepped in and paid to repair and replace our fence, clean out the mold, and rebuild the front pillars, which allowed us to move back into our home.

Our insurance had not yet kicked in, so we could only live in the left side of the home. On the right side, the floors were gone and even the sheetrock had come down. For the month after the tornado, FEMA (the Federal Emergency Management Agency) sent in big disaster trucks filled with food; they set up in the parking lot of what used to be the church next door. We were fed all three meals each day.

About two weeks later, we went to the Salvation Army because we needed some cleaning supplies. When we got there, a woman said, "We have boxes of clothes. Do you need clothes?" I remember looking up at this lady; she was so nice, and I just started crying. I said, "I don't have anything. I don't have anything left." She told me I survived for a purpose and asked if she could pray with me. Afterward I, in turn, asked if I could hug her. "Of course," she said. It was a healing hug. That's why every time I see someone, I hug them. I know how to recognize pain.

"What do you want? Do you want a purse?" she asked me. I just kept crying in her arms. She held me, and we prayed. "It's going to be okay," she told me over and over. I left with a bunch of things that were not covered by insurance—a kitchen table, stools, dishes, household decor, blankets, comforters, towels, and a love seat. And she put together a basket of other necessities like small soaps, shampoos, conditioners, toothpaste, and toothbrushes.

Seeing how the community came together to help us and other victims of the tornado made me want to give back someday when we were back on our feet.

In a way, the tornado was both an end and a new beginning.

PART THREE

2016 to Present

12

Breaking from My Past

Though I was still shaken by our brush with death, Gerardo and I continued to be uplifted by the outpouring of love from perfect strangers that came to us in the wake of that devastating tornado. For months afterward, our local gas stations, nearby convenience clerks, and neighbors greeted each other in a more friendly manner. They were more considerate and sensitive to each other—we had survived together, and it had created a deep sense of community.

Repairs were slow going, and I began to sink into depression and despair, staring at our destroyed home and having lost Alan to what would continue to be a very unstable life with Amanda. Their rental hadn't worked out, so they moved back home with us, as if we didn't have enough stress with the aftermath of the tornado. By early spring of 2016, Alan and Amanda decided to move to a luxurious apartment complex to live with Amanda's best friend and her husband. Amanda demanded name-brand furniture and other luxuries they couldn't afford, which Alan put on credit cards, sinking him deeper and deeper into debt. Alan was always sacrificing for others, and just like me, he'd learned to never say no to his controlling, angry partner.

That living situation lasted less than six months. Amanda's drinking led to fights with her roommates, so that September they moved in with Amanda's mother, which didn't go well either. That January, Alan called Gerardo to ask if they could move back in with us. Amanda had gotten into a violent altercation with her sister and had been arrested. He'd just bailed her out of jail. We reluctantly agreed. How could we refuse to help our son?

It didn't take long for tension to build up again. Amanda had no respect toward me in particular. She would not do her share of household chores, so I was dealing with sinks full of dishes and her screaming and yelling at my son. It took a toll on my emotional well-being. Amanda thought we should cater to her every whim, and all the while she disrespected my family home. I sank deeper and deeper into despair.

I was struggling with what I was witnessing. We had lovingly opened our home to Amanda many times, and I understood—perhaps better than anyone—that she was going through her own pain. I don't know if she was able to see that we had allowed her to come into our home because we cared deeply for our son. There were all sorts of things I dealt with that I disagreed with, but we had to remain quiet for Alan. Unfortunately, we did not know how to handle the situation any better; we weren't equipped for it.

I had to face the pain of a mother seeing her son emotionally abused. We observed a lot of alcohol abuse and heard her yelling and swearing at Alan when they fought. It was not what

I had envisioned for my son, yet they say no good deed goes unpunished. Gerardo too realized that letting them live with us had been a total mistake. We should have asked them to save their own money and pay their own expenses until they could afford their own home. We should have set limits and boundaries.

This was tearing me apart. When I started a conversation, Amanda offered little attention and absolutely no empathy. I often got the silent treatment. Perhaps her way of trying to brush off all the trauma that she had suffered was making us the targets of her wrath. I was in a state of emotional chaos and turmoil in my own home. I began to experience panic attacks. My emotional distress was so great that I would stay in my room to avoid seeing my son being yelled at.

I suppose she, in her own way, cared for him. But she also knew how to hurt others, how to hurt me the most. I endured all the pain for the sake of my son. I knew there was nothing I could do or say, because they were in love. I also knew that my son was going to suffer, and he began to blame me for the tension between us. Unfortunately, as I know from firsthand experience, a person cannot see the harmful effects of a toxic relationship while it's happening. Yet I still hold no resentment because I know in my heart she was only repeating dysfunctional generational patterns passed along by her mother or father.

To this day, we love our son dearly, and he loves us. Deep down, I know nothing can truly separate us.

***

One day in April 2017, I was on the internet, literally shaking from anxiety about the ongoing situation with Amanda, so I googled online counselors, and from there, in the midst of my pain, reached out to several therapists who offered remote therapy sessions via Skype. That's how I found my counselor, Renee, who showed me compassion and began to empower me. She was a faith-based counselor but didn't push her faith on her patients. Instead, she asked, "May I pray for you?" during one of my first sessions.

I embraced the fact that Renee did not impose her faith. Rather, she made sure she asked in a manner that left it completely up to me to choose to allow it or not. Unlike my mother and all the men who imposed their will by physical force, manipulation, or psychological damage, Renee was a kind and benevolent person who genuinely had my best interests at heart. I had never experienced this type of pure divine love, and she truly touched the root of my emotional pain. I'm so grateful I found her, because not long after we connected, Amanda and I had our worst confrontation yet.

One afternoon, I walked into my laundry room and saw her there, so I asked her to help out with household tasks and clean up after herself. I just wanted her to do her share. She began yelling aggressively at me; I will never forget the hatred in her eyes. She raised her hand, and at that point, I knew she was capable of physical violence. I was terrified. I knew how bad her temper was, so I ran to my bedroom. Gerardo was on his way home from his trucking job, which he'd kept while we were rebuilding our real estate careers and my insurance business. I was in our bedroom, trembling and in agony from back pain triggered by the stress. I was so angry at my son's girlfriend. Then, I looked at my nightstand and saw the OxyContin I was still taking.

I am not saying that it was Amanda's fault. It was not Amanda's fault. It was my own issues. The confrontations with her triggered memories of Cesar's beatings, which made me just want to end the pain once and for all.

I started gulping down OxyContin two at a time. Suddenly I heard a noise outside my back door. Gerardo was home. Worried about how Gerardo would react, I ran to our bathroom, put my finger in my mouth, and began throwing up the pills into the toilet. As Gerardo walked into our bathroom, he found me hanging over the toilet bowl, shaking and crying unconsolably. Worried that I hadn't gotten all the drugs out of my system, I asked him to take me to the hospital and to text Renee.

"You do not need to go to a hospital," he said in a dismissive tone. I was still not driving, and I was in no shape to do so anyway, so I told him I would call 911. Gerardo never liked me calling the police. I wonder if this man would have let me die. I don't want to think so. I prefer to think that it was just ignorance, that maybe he thought because I'd survived my last overdose attempt without going to the hospital, I didn't need to go now. Nevertheless, after I threatened to call the police, he reluctantly agreed to take me himself but didn't text Renee for me.

She was my only lifeline at that time, so I texted her on the way to the hospital to tell her what I'd taken and that I was feeling suicidal. It was around 5:00 p.m., but she quickly texted me back to say she was with a patient and I should seek immediate help. I told her I was on my way to the hospital. The drive there seemed to take forever. I kept seeing my life playing over and over in my head, like a movie: my mother's neglect and inability to love me, the sexual abuse when I was a child, the beatings and kidnapping by Cesar, the strict and misogynistic rules Charles enforced, feeling trapped and unloved by Gerardo, the ongoing conflict with Amanda. I'd just hit rock bottom. It was so painful. We arrived at the emergency entrance for Garland Behavioral Hospital. Coincidentally, this hospital was the very same one to which Cesar had brought me when he'd viciously broken my nose when I was a teen. This in itself triggered more traumatic memories of all that I had endured at his hands.

They immediately checked me in to pump my stomach, but I told them I thought that I had thrown up everything. I was frantic and terrified. At the same time, I was crying inconsolably to the nurses, telling them about my husband's emotional coldness, how he was unable to set firm boundaries and standards in our home with my son and Amanda. All this stress and anxiety came bubbling out, but it was not my latest confrontation with Amanda that led to my suicide attempt. I knew that. It was the culmination of everything that had happened before that.

**

I stayed at Garland Hospital for several hours while I was assessed to see if I needed to be transferred to a long-term mental health facility. Nurses took my vitals, blood, and urine. I spoke to counselors about what had happened; then a doctor came in and told me I was going to be involuntarily committed. I was stunned. I'd thought I'd come to the hospital to get help. I hadn't expected to be imprisoned. It felt unspeakably cruel. I had no history of violence. I was just a woman who was going through a terrible time, and now I couldn't leave? I'd had no idea I could be committed to a hospital against my will for a suicide attempt. The process took me totally by surprise.

I was strapped to a gurney so I couldn't move my arms and legs, moved into an ambulance, and transported to Sundance

Behavioral and Mental Health Hospital, an inpatient treatment center. I cannot tell you how terrifying that drive was for me, though it was only a few miles. I had committed no crime, but I felt like a prisoner, a criminal. To this day just thinking about that awful ambulance ride can send me into a panic attack.

Once I arrived at Sundance, all my belongings were searched by female guards at the facility, and I began going through the intake process, which took several hours. They locked me in a small evaluation room. The white steel doors were dirty. The floor seemed to be mopped; however, the janitorial staff could not keep up with the influx of patients. Through the windows in the room, I saw a young lady being wheeled in on a stretcher, escorted by police officers. Both her wrists were sutured. Seeing her lying there like that is something I will never forget. I must have seen at least seven people in various stages of distress come in for treatment that day.

After several hours and another evaluation, a nurse came in to tell me I was being admitted; then she escorted me to the seventh floor. There was a corridor that divided the men's and women's patient sections. All my personal belongings were seized by the hospital staff and stored away. I was issued a caddy container with basic essentials like a toothbrush, toothpaste, shampoo, a comb, and a few other items, but that was it. Along the way, I made a stop at the nurses' station to sign in, and I placed Gerardo's number on the list so that I could contact him. Then I sat on a chair in the hallway until I was assigned a room, which I would share with four women.

The horror show continued. Nurses escorted a young man who couldn't have been more than twenty-five down the hall, but he fell down in front of me. They slapped him on the face to try to get him to wake up, but he didn't respond. I started panicking. Two older orderlies rushed in to help the nurses, but they couldn't get him to respond either. They dragged him to another part of the hospital. Some of the other patients later told me that the young man had overdosed on heroin. He survived but had partial brain damage.

Next, I saw a young woman with bruises on her legs, arms, and face. A man wearing a black jacket was screaming at her. She yelled at the staff and became physically aggressive. A nurse quickly applied a restraint hold and strapped her to the gurney so they could sedate her; then he and another nurse took her to her room. This young lady had been drugged against her will. To me, she looked dead. What is the difference between legal and illegal drugs? It didn't seem like there was much of a difference to me.

The system is so broken. These souls needed love and compassion, and instead they got violence. Childhood traumas and our system's mental health facilities need more awareness and programming on how trauma impacts a child's life. More must be done to make a difference instead of medicating or misdiagnosing people who, like me, simply need love and compassion.

I found out later that the young woman was a sex worker who had been beaten by her pimp for not bringing in the amount of money that he required. She came in under the influence of some illegal drug and needing help, and she was drugged with something else so she'd remain asleep all day.

Such exploitation, such injustice, such oppression of women.

This is the moment the seed of my passion for women's ministry was planted.

I could not believe what I was seeing in a place I had come to for help. What awful thing would happen next? The staff seemed to have no compassion. At the slightest sign of resistance, they'd threaten to give you a shot of what the longer-term patients called booty juice, a sedative that was given via a shot in the buttocks, which I assumed is what they'd forced on the young woman I'd seen earlier.

I was given a tour, and the staff explained the rules of the facility at length, as well as the levels of disciplinary actions for breaking the rules. We had set schedules to see psychiatrists and psychologists and participate in daily activities, which included group counseling. We were all on a behavior scale, which rewarded good behavior with extra privileges like TV time and use of the telephone. Some patients had an extremely low tolerance for frustration and would verbally assault the hospital staff. These women were not provided privileges. They would sometimes have to be confined to their rooms to eat, and they were not allowed to eat in the cafeteria or go outside during recreation time.

Most of the patients were drug addicts, sex workers, and former inmates. I could see stories of horrific abuse in all the women's faces, and I felt such empathy for them when they shared their stories. I could relate to their pain because I had lived the same pain. I loved these souls, and that is where my desire to fight for women's rights was born.

Despite some of the horrific treatment of patients I witnessed at Sundance, I had good therapists and learned in group sessions that I was not the only woman who had been sexually molested as a child or endured domestic violence as an adult. I began to feel something inside, something growing out of my soul like that first flower bud of spring, pushing through the snow. I felt a new purpose light a fire within me: I could be a mother to the motherless, to the hurting, to the crushed, and to the oppressed. This feeling was like a cocoon where Little Nikki was beginning to heal and grow. The truths and kind words we shared with each other filled me with a bright, healing light, and Little Nikki made a breakthrough. She was capable of loving others and began separating herself from the stifled and scared little girl she'd been all her life. I had found the beginning of my true life's purpose, to be of service to other women in pain.

I befriended many of the women, even the hard-core girls who had done prison time—I called them my soul sisters. At first, they were distant, but I won them over. Maybe they could tell I truly cared for them and saw them as real people. The truth is, I realized I could have easily been them. In many ways, I *was* them. We had different ethnicities, cultures, and family histories, but we all shared one thing in common: we had all been through some painful abuse and trauma. We had to learn to forgive, to not allow this painful trauma to have power over us. This was the beginning of that process for me.

I stayed there for less than a week. Renee somehow broke through the bureaucratic red tape and arranged to have me released early.

"Well, you did it, kiddo. You're a survivor," a nurse told me with a smile as I was packing to leave. I started crying. A simple act of compassion begins with reaching out to an unloved soul. I told her I'd never come back—unless it was to share my story.

I knew I couldn't go back to a home where Amanda lived, so I put some of my newfound strength and inner knowing to the test. I asked Gerardo to choose: Alan and Amanda or me. Gerardo told Alan he could stay but that Amanda had to leave.

She was gone by the time I came home.

13

New Horizons, New Life

When did I lose my voice? How have I arrived at such despair in my life? I've lost my autonomy. All these thoughts ran through my head as I steeled myself to leave the hospital, a place that, after my initial shock, had become a sanctuary of sorts. Amanda may have left our home, but I was still going to be a prisoner of Gerardo, of his rules and control.

The one thing I'd learned was that there was no more running; there was no other way but through that deep pain inside myself. I'd begun to think more clearly after being away from the toxic environment in my home. Things had to change. I was determined to take control of my life. I was determined to regain my identity, to live a purposeful and meaningful life, so I decided to re-create my self-image. In short, I came home with a whole new perspective.

I knew I needed something more in my life, something spiritual, especially after what I had witnessed at Sundance. I still felt such a deep void in my heart, one I knew the Catholic church could not fill. I just did not feel any warmth, any fellowship, or any love at the Catholic church. Before my suicide attempt, I'd asked Gerardo for permission to attend New Life Church, which had at first appealed to me because it was so close to our home.

Instead, he said he would find a new church for us. He too had felt let down by the Catholic church. A few weeks before my suicide attempt, he'd gone to the church to ask for the priest's help with me because I'd begged and pleaded with him to do so, but he'd been told the priest's schedule was full. Gerardo had been able to convince the church secretary to book him an appointment with a deacon, but Gerardo'd had to pay him to do so.

The deacon had showed up at our home one day the following week. He'd been limping, and he'd appeared to be in physical pain. It had been clear to me he hadn't wanted to be there. In fact, he'd told me he had been commanded to come, even though he was in no shape to do so. He'd recited the rosary, but there'd been no compassion or hope in his words. He'd told me I had to get rid of the "cobwebs" of my negative thoughts before I could be helped. In that moment I thought of Renee and her kind, easy, nonjudgmental way of faith. She always seemed happy and joyful and was able to connect with me on a deeper spiritual level by the way she wove scripture into our sessions.

In my desperation, I'd tried so many things over the years to ease my pain. I'd sought shamans, New Age wisdom, and many types of alternate healings. You name it, I tried it. But I found that none of these connected me with my creator. One day Gerardo was listening to a Spanish radio station and learned about Templo de Dios, a miracle healing ministry. He thought maybe that would be a good new church for us; perhaps they could heal my wounds. At this point, anything was worth a try, so I agreed to go with him.

At first the pastoral congregation seemed to be the perfect match. It was where I met my friend Joanie. We were at a Father's Day celebration at the church in 2017 when I saw her, a young mother sitting alone with her four-month-old daughter. I introduced myself, and we bonded instantly. I came to see her as the daughter I never had and her husband, Franco, as my son.

It wasn't long, though, before I figured out that this church was more like a cult. I really liked some of the members and asked if they wanted to go out to dinner, but they said they had to ask the pastor first. I couldn't believe it. The church would tell us it wasn't good for us to get together outside of church events because it would cause problems, that the women would start gossiping, and the pastor didn't like gossip. We also weren't allowed to spend time with people who didn't belong to the church.

I began noticing how the pastor twisted scripture, using sacred biblical texts and teachings to suggest requirements of obedience to an abuser. This in turn produced feelings of isolation for the victim and justification for their punishment, and reinforced the abuser's belief in their own superiority and elitism. He was nothing more than a false teacher with a grandiose personality. It was even reflected in his own marriage. His wife used the same toxic, cruel, coercive control tactics to subdue the congregation members. I also learned that the pastor, who had plenty of money, demanded some of his congregants work for him for free, including the husband of one of my friends. In addition, every year, in January, the pastor and his wife collected a specific lump sum of money called *primicias* from all the congregants, which they said would make sure each family was blessed the entire year. This requirement is not found in the Bible but rather was a mandate made by this pastor. And it was in addition to the *diezmo*, or 10 percent tithe, that was required each month. Despite all that money coming in, the pastor and his wife did not do anything that their nonprofit claimed to, such as helping orphans and widows. I knew this was not a healthy or safe place for me or my family to grow spiritually.

Then Joanie told me a male teacher was sending inappropriate texts to some of the teen girls. When I spoke to the pastor about my concerns, he twisted the conversation, ending up cursing my relationship with Gerardo, saying I would lose him if I kept blaspheming against the Holy Spirit. I told him that I felt he was leading the members with toxic leadership, which other women had complained about as well. But he wouldn't listen. I left ashamed, hurt, in pain and tears, confused—I was in such a frantic state. I had intervened for another church member and ended up being chastised by the pastor. My needs and those of the congregation were not important to him. I immediately sought Renee's counsel and therapy, and she validated my concerns.

Gerardo, not surprisingly, was not happy I had confronted the pastor. He too had a distorted view of God, and it was very obvious he and his pastor had common ground; what was lord over both their lives was money. They both also loved and craved admiration and used manipulation to control people. I'd had it, and in October 2019, I mustered enough strength to stand up to Gerardo and say, "I refuse to go to this church. And I will attend New Life Church instead. I want to."

So that's how I began attending New Life, which totally changed my life. One Sunday, the pastor, Pastor Stanley, invited those who wanted to make a new spiritual commitment to Jesus Christ to come to the altar in what is called an altar call. I accepted the invitation. One after another, older women began to touch my shoulders and pray. I began crying and crying and crying. I must have cried a million tears for every wound in my life. This was like nothing I'd ever experienced. I felt a warm, healing, sublime energy as if jolts of love were being sent to me. It was a force stronger than anything I'd ever experienced. I call it the Divine Touch. When I got up from the floor, I hugged two of the mother-like figures. Each hug felt like a soothing balm to my traumatic past, my deeply wounded soul; their love felt like the maternal love I'd been yearning for my entire life.

I began to look forward to each Sunday-morning service, even while fighting with Gerardo over his refusal to accept that I was healing and his ongoing resistance to me attending this church. Many times, I questioned myself. I'd heard Gerardo tell me time and time again that God was in heaven. But through these older women, I'd witnessed truly divine love.

They became my spiritual mothers. They must have seen Little Nikki in me, that timid little girl, the broken child who'd been emotionally stifled. I remained stuck in time, I suppose, back to when Cesar had abducted me, or maybe it went back to when my mother had abused me. Perhaps I was, in a way, stuck in all those moments of trauma, never really able to be in the present moment. At altar call each Sunday, the motherly women greeted me with hugs. Each time I went up to the pulpit, I saw them as mothers, praying, holding hands. It was as if I were making up for all those years of neglect, all the hugs Mom should have given me ever since the moment I was born.

I know now love heals like nothing else. God is love. I am

also aware today that what one person calls spiritual abuse may to another be no more than a disagreement. I had already been down this path during my marriage to Charles, where he followed the belief from his church about women needing to submit to a man's authority. In the end, I had not felt love when I'd attended Charles's church. I had not felt love at Gerardo's cultish church. It was at New Life Church that I was opened to the possibility and full extent of true love.

Gerardo decided to attend New Life Church with me, but he still went to the other one as well. For a while, things stabilized a bit. I was able to focus on myself and my personal and spiritual growth. But then the other shoe dropped.

Come Christmastime that year, New Life was holding a donation drive for people in other countries who needed Bibles. I wrote a check for $700, but I needed Gerardo's signature, as all our accounts were in his name. At first he'd said yes, but then he changed his mind, refusing to sign the check. He told me he saw no need to help this church because "they have more money" than his other church.

I could do nothing. I cried all night, sad, exhausted, and then angry as I realized I had absolutely no power over my situation. I could not fulfill the pledge I'd made to God from the bottom of my heart, all because I had no control over my finances. I did not have any bank accounts in my name. I had put forth at least half the work in creating our real estate business, yet he had structured the business so that he was the sole owner. He controlled everything, including me. I had no identity.

But as my tears dried up, I realized it didn't always have to be this way. I could take control; I could make the decisions for my future. I decided in that moment: I would form my own small women's ministry.

***

One of the few good things that had come out of going to Templo de Dios was my friendship with Joanie and Franco. After I settled in at New Life, Franco suggested I get more spiritual guidance from his half sister, Sandy, who was a volunteer at a church in Houston, Texas.

Franco and Joanie invited Gerardo and me to Lakewood Church, where Sandy served as a ministry volunteer, and that introduction birthed a new hope. She told me she'd recently had to end her in-home women's ministry that helped other women find their purpose. She said she'd found it so fulfilling. That epiphany I'd had came back to me—here was something I could do.

Not long afterward, I created my own small ministry, with a handful of women, including Joanie and her mother, Tammy, as well as Tessi, a loan officer I knew. We all began attending Sandy's Zoom Bible classes every Tuesday at lunchtime, which helped my faith become stronger and stronger. Sandy empowered us with the word of God, which allowed me to address my repressed anger. Sandy would often offer counsel, and she would share biblical scriptures speaking of forgiveness. I began to draw on her spiritual strength. I began to see that the Bible was the only way I could find truth in the midst of my pain and chaos.

I also drew strength from my friendships with the women in my ministry. We each came from different walks of life, but we came together to form tight bonds. All the women were trauma survivors, so we all understood where the others were coming from. I could see my pain served a purpose now. How else would I have had compassion great enough that I could identify with and care lovingly for the pain, shame, and guilt my soul sisters were experiencing? They all needed a mother, a mentor, a word of encouragement. One thing was for sure: they too were facing their own battles and struggles in their relationships. Yet we empowered each other. We complemented each other.

Together, we would read books and talk about what was going on in our lives—we still check in on each other every week. Tammy works three jobs, and the last time we caught up, she told me she'd left her husband. I said, "You're going to get through this," and she just hugged me.

I know no one is perfect, but I embrace my friends, even those who have hurt or betrayed me; they are all a part of my journey. We are all travelers, and I see their actions as lessons that help me grow, both spiritually and emotionally.

14

Open the Floodgates

After Gerardo refused to sign the $700 check for New Life Church, I realized I needed to free myself from his financial control. I started doing some cold-calling as well as reaching out to my old contacts from the real estate world to try to drum up new business.

One day in late 2020, I got a call from a real estate investor, Al, expressing interest in buying a house that I had listed for a relative of his. Gerardo would often list me as a second real estate agent so I could take his calls if he wasn't available. This time I was beyond happy I'd gotten the call, because Al was a top dog in real estate and told me if I sold the home to him, he would introduce me to wholesaling—basically flipping private off-market properties and homes for one or more of his companies. He knew Dallas was a hot market where home prices had risen dramatically despite the pandemic, due to short supply and high demand.

I immediately knew this was my chance to break out on my own. Some might call it luck, but I call it destiny. We are all travelers, and we will meet with fate along our journey, if only we are ready to reach out and grab it. I believe we are not alone on this journey; there is always an opportunity or a person ready to lift us up and help us to the next step on our ladder.

Toward the end of our twenty-minute conversation, I told Al I had been doing real estate for close to two decades now, but I wanted to begin flipping homes so I could go out on my own. He offered me full price in cash for the home and told me if I sold it to him, he'd introduce me to his team as family. "But where will I get the money to buy these houses?" I asked. He said he'd put me in touch with a personal assistant who was a hard money lender who could help me finance house flipping.

I gave him the contract and accepted his offer. We closed within two weeks. For the next month or so, I thought about Al's promise, then finally decided to call and ask him if he still planned to introduce me to the real estate flipping market. He sounded like he was in a rush and told me he was about to catch an international flight. I pressed on anyway, asking, "Al, did you really mean what you said?"

"Call my assistant," he told me. "They have your name and all you need to begin your career as the next successful real estate flipper." He told me he'd check back in with me in two weeks to see if I had everything I needed.

I was on cloud nine. Though he was a busy man, Al kept his promise, and I was soon learning the ins and outs of the flipping business. I knew that Father God had sent him as a helper to fulfill my purpose in this life. And by God, when he opens a door—trust me, no mortal man can close it. My pain was all part of a divine plan that had been arranged in the book of life. God had been preparing to give me a testimony that I might shed light on the gospel of Jesus.

Next up was taking back control over my life and finances. Gerardo had initially set up a business LLC under his name because his credit was better than mine, but I finally told Gerardo I wanted my name on it too. I took back my dignity, and I stood up for all that I deserved. It was time; in fact, it was long overdue. We'd built this business together, and I deserved to have that acknowledgment and control. He kept putting me off, though, until the issues in our marriage came to a head in July 2021.

Gerardo told me he wanted to shoot his gun in the air to celebrate the Fourth of July, which is a tradition in the Mexican culture for both July Fourth and New Year's Eve celebrations. It honestly caught me off guard, because he hadn't touched his gun for some time. Anxiety immediately rose up in me, and I felt unsafe. I grabbed my keys and told Gerardo I was going to file a police report about his plans to fire his gun.

As I was driving there, Gerardo called and told me he was going to add me to the LLC and also help me set up my own checking and savings accounts. He promised to do all this before we left for our planned vacation to Cancún in late July. Of course, he was only doing this as a bargaining chip, to stop me from filing the report. But I realized I had to take this opportunity before Gerardo changed his mind. I set up an appointment at Bank of America, and for the first time in my marriage, I got a checking and savings account solely in my name. Though there were times in our marriage when we'd had joint accounts, I honestly cannot recall ever having my own checking account.

I also asked Gerardo to set up an appointment with his

attorney to review the company's documents. The attorney explained he could add me on to the company in less than a week, and I was quickly added as a co-owner of the business. We were now equal owners.

It took great strength to face the giants that I had been up against, but I managed to take back what was rightfully mine.

**

It was as if all this decisive action had ripped the Band-Aid off, had uncorked the dam. I felt powerful and ready to confront every part of my past—no matter how painful. I requested a copy of the police report that had been filed when Cesar had beaten me so brutally in April 1984. I also filed a separate complaint against him for the kidnapping I'd endured.

We were at the Dallas–Fort Worth airport on our way back from Cancún in July when I got a message from the Garland police saying they'd found the 1984 police report. I asked Gerardo to rush there so I could pick it up. I don't think I'd ever seen it.

I was holding it in my hand when flashbacks to that terrible night pierced my brain. I could hear and feel Cesar viciously breaking my nose, hitting me so hard I had woken up with contusions and bruises all over my body as well as a broken front tooth. It had been a beating that had scarred me emotionally and psychologically for most of my life and always brought me back to the kidnapping and horrific abuse I'd endured at Cesar's hands.

As I began reading that police report, I noticed it was a "citation." Cesar had brutally beaten me and received a mere citation! Anger rose up in me. There was no justice for a young girl who had no one standing up for her. No parents. No family. No friends. No financial resources. And when I had been released from the hospital, the only place I'd had to go back to was Mary's house, the same person who would later help Cesar kidnap me at knifepoint and smuggle me into Mexico.

As I held the police report, I noticed Gerardo was getting uneasy. I wondered if he was still worried I would go to the police about him. Our trip to Cancún had left me more frightened of him than ever. He'd gotten upset when I'd gone out to see a show with my niece one night, and we had a confrontation about my fear of his threatening to shoot off his gun over Fourth of July a few weeks before. After our confrontation, he'd forced me to have anal sex with him. Gerardo had reluctantly agreed to start going to therapy again when we returned, but I was skeptical. I did not believe Gerardo could change in the way I, especially as the new person I was trying to become, needed him to for our marriage to work. And I was done letting him get his way. As a result, there was even more tension and friction in our relationship than ever.

I realized that Gerardo was an angry man, though, and that leaving him could place me in danger. Once alone, I called my friend Sandy, nearly hysterical, and told her that I now had money to leave Gerardo but felt my life could be in danger if I tried to do so. She told me that I needed to calm down, that it was best to leave Gerardo gradually rather than going straight to no contact. I heeded her words and made plans to fly to Houston in early August to visit with her and look for a place to live.

During my visit, Sandy helped me look for apartments and guided me to read scripture, all of which brought me peace and made me feel empowered. I'd never had a friend as wise as her, and I realized the advice she gave me was prudent. When I returned home, I told Gerardo that we had real problems and that I wanted a separation to give our relationship time to heal.

He agreed and came to the Houston area with me to pick out a place for me to live. Because I had no proof of income (Gerardo had filed all the tax returns in his name only), Gerardo had to sign the lease as well, which is perhaps why he wasn't that upset when I asked for the separation. He knew he still had control over me. Later, he also hired a moving company to move all my belongings, and as I still wasn't comfortable driving long distances on my own, I depended on him for that as well.

We officially signed the lease on September 15, 2021, for a 1,044-square-foot two-bedroom apartment with granite counters, hardwood floors, and a patio where I couldn't wait to relax outside. The rent was $1,656 a month. The complex was a fifty-five-plus community, but the manager made an exception for me since I was younger at the time, and I was so grateful. There was a pool, a gym, and even a beauty salon on site. It was close to shops and restaurants and just outside Houston. Most importantly, it was nearly four hours away from Garland, where Gerardo still lived, which gave me the space I needed.

The arrangement worked well, and he respected my boundaries. However, I knew in my heart that he was unpredictable. I had wanted a two-bedroom for when he visited, as I'd told him I would not have sex with him while we were separated. But I didn't yet have the courage to tell him the thought of him coming near me made me nauseated.

***

It felt strange sleeping alone my very first night in the apartment. Yet it was also as if a huge burden had lifted, not just from Gerardo but from work pressures as well, since he was always pushing me to work more hours and make more money. For the first time, I was practicing self-care. Learning to say no was hard—something I still sometimes struggle with—but it was so important. It is a small word, but it is packed with loads of power. I learned saying no meant saying yes to myself—to self-love, self-power, and self-control.

I set strict boundaries about communication with toxic family and friends who did not have my best interests at heart. These boundaries not only gave me control of my time, but they also freed up my mental space and energy. A big flaw that I'd always struggled with was giving too much of myself, wanting to please others, and needing external validation from others. Most importantly, setting boundaries relieved the societal pressure that brought loads of unneeded stress into my daily life. I lived in a beautiful area surrounded by huge pine trees, and I traded stress for simple things, like a daily walk exploring the area, reading a good book on the patio, or taking a bubble bath.

My downtime became so important to me. Saying no allowed me to free up time to work on my writing and focus on other projects that I was excited about. It even reenergized me. One of my first projects was furnishing my apartment. I decorated it tastefully with some midcentury furniture, along with towels, linens, bedding, and beautiful rugs from a local shop. I'd never had so much independence, so much freedom to choose what *I* liked. Releasing those pent-up pressures and finding relief from stress was exhilarating! I began to truly heal.

Gerardo visited on the weekends, as he'd signed the lease with the condition that we would attend church, including their deliverance classes. But otherwise, I was living alone for the first time in my life. Waking up alone. Eating alone. Much to my surprise, I enjoyed my solitude. I had Rocky, who was now fourteen years old, to keep me company, and I enjoyed having my space to journal and read daily scripture meditations. Before, I'd always been scared of being alone, but now I embraced and cherished my solitude.

Being away from Gerardo also helped me kick my addiction to opioids once and for all. The long walks helped me with my back pain, so I hadn't been taking as many, but I still relied on them. One night, I happened upon a documentary about the opioid crisis on TV. I was horrified. I'd trusted my mental and physical health and well-being to doctors and psychiatrists, but I'd failed to research all the anxiety and other opioid medications that they'd put me on. I did not realize how harmful and addictive opioids were or the long-term effects of withdrawal. And my doctors had been more than willing to overprescribe.

I used some of my newfound free time to do research about opioids. I found out that the fentanyl patches I had used had some serious potential side effects and that they could be habit forming. I'd had no idea, but I've since learned to be more careful about what I allow into my body. My doctor started weaning me off medications after I demanded more information about my treatment options. I still need medication for some of the nerve problems that stem from my back injuries caused by the car accidents, but I was able to break free from the opioid addiction.

Now I just had to see if I could truly break free of Gerardo.

I was determined to face every adversity head-on. I was going to stand up for Little Nikki and protect her above everything else. I was going to give her a safe space to grow and smile, and I was going to learn to reparent her.

Until this point, Gerardo had very skillfully destroyed

every attempt I'd made to have friends. No more. I empowered myself by having multiple consultations with attorneys via Zoom about my situation. Though we'd been living together for all those years, I learned that Gerardo and I had been legally divorced since 2000. I have always believed I was free, and now I've learned to express it.

The uneasy truce between Gerardo and me is now over, and he no longer visits me at my apartment. I still need to separate myself from him financially, which is more complicated than I thought. But I refuse to back down. Not this time. Not ever again.

15

The Trauma Stops Here

As I was struggling to become who I wanted to be, I began to think about my mother's half brother, Uncle Victor, who had been in prison for as long as I could remember. He was serving a ninety-nine-year prison sentence for burglary and other convictions. Having lived my own life of confinement, I could truly identify with him. I had not been in an actual prison, of course, but I had still been in a psychological one, serving a term I had self-imposed by chaining my life and worth to Gerardo.

I had fond memories of Victor. He had been good to his girlfriend, bringing her teddy bears and flowers; he'd loved to play his guitar; and he'd always brought my brothers and me candy. I hoped he could help fill in some gaps in my knowledge about our family's violent past and the circumstances that led to the untimely deaths of so many in our bloodline.

I also wanted to share my newfound faith journey with Victor. All his life he'd been an outcast. Based on conversations I'd had with my mother in the past, it seemed everyone had just ignored and judged my uncle based on his actions. I wanted him to learn that God had touched my life and that I was no longer embarrassed or ashamed to reach out to him. I wrote letters to him, and he filled me in on some shocking family secrets. I developed compassion toward my uncle after he shared that he had been in some physical fights in prison. He apologized and said he'd understand if I no longer wanted to communicate with him. He appeared to be ashamed of his actions, though, and I knew shame all too well. I encouraged him to seek out more knowledge in the Bible and began to exchange spiritual teachings with him. I wanted to reconnect with him.

I discovered my uncle, just like me, had witnessed trauma early on as a child. He had witnessed domestic violence when his biological father had beaten my grandma. He said, "I was standing up to him at such a young age," perhaps even as early as he can remember, between five and eight years old. I began to realize that, more often than not, abuse experienced during childhood affects one's life well into adulthood.

When we are abused as kids, we may find it difficult to walk down the better path when faced with a choice at a crossroads later in life. As Victor filled in more details about my family, I began to see a generational pattern that turned deadly, leading to multiple deaths and murders in my family. Some might call it a family curse. For example, my mother's aunt, who'd experienced domestic violence, had gone on to kill two of her partners. Why? I believe it was because of the anger and bitterness that had manifested in her because she had been abused by those men. To this day, women have seen justice fail them time after time, as was the case for me, my mother, my grandma, and so many others. My mother's aunt had taken justice into her own hands, and while the outcome was terrible, who could blame her?

My uncle helped me understand our family's tortured history. Because so many in my family on my maternal grandmother's side had harbored bitterness, it had taken root and led to anger and violence. The only way to deal with it and stop the cycle was by turning that bitterness over to a higher source. It had to be laid to rest.

And there was no better place to start than with my mother.

***

I truly wanted to let go of my anger and bitterness toward my mother, though I must confess it is easier said than done when someone has hurt you so deeply.

After my grandmother died in September 2014, we got into our worst argument yet, at one of Julie's cookouts. I don't remember what started it, but I blurted out, "You never cared about me!" and she told me I should be grateful she'd raised me and hadn't given me away. I told her that it would have been better growing up with an adoptive family than to have faced all her physical and emotional abuse, that Grandma had told me she'd begged Julie to keep me, and that I knew I was a child of rape. She got so angry she told me to take my children and leave, which is what we did. Our relationship was even more strained after that. We didn't speak at all for the following eight months and then lapsed into an uneasy estrangement.

The first step to recovery was to acknowledge that hurt—that it was real and that it had adversely affected my life. Second, I decided to quit nursing the resentment that I had held toward her for so many years. As I thought about Mom's influence and how her shadow had followed me throughout my life, I honestly felt it was because I had not forgiven her. Being near her made me anxious, and all I wanted to do was flee every time I knew she would be around. That fight-or-flight response is normal, I suppose. Our subconscious has a way of recording everything, the good, the bad, and all that we live through. It was now time to let all that go and allow Little Nikki to grow into the beautiful, strong, confident woman that I knew I was.

Forgiving the ones who had harmed me was the hardest thing for me to do. Yet I had to forgive my aggressors. I had to work through that pain. There was no other escape route. I had to go through the pain. I guess I had been running away from it all my life, and it had finally caught up with me. It was the hardest thing for me to do, yet once I did it, I promised myself I would never go that route again.

So, in August 2021, after years of estrangement, I got my mother's phone number from Junior, whom she texted at times, and called her. We spoke for more than two hours. I discovered she was living with a man who physically and psychologically abused her. Her boyfriend, Ken, had had an honorable discharge from the US Air Force, but he'd quickly become an alcoholic. She said his drinking was out of control and that she'd even had to call the police on him recently.

After she'd told me some of the things Ken had done, I asked her why she didn't move in with Rob, my brother with whom she was still close, and she admitted it was because she

depended on Ken financially. I understood completely. I told
her a bit about my situation and how I'd experienced some
similar things.

The worst part was my mom did not see herself as an
abused woman. She had been in this abusive relationship for
over five years, yet she thought she deserved the treatment and
cruelty. I wanted to empower her and told her she didn't need
to stay in this type of relationship. I explained what financial
abuse and control are, that they are psychologically harmful,
and that I knew all about it firsthand. Yet she was trapped in a
giant mental prison of her own making. She did not want to go
through processing the pain, guilt, and shame that she carried
in order to be free. I told her she needed help spiritually, which
she could get by attending a church.

The first time I saw her in person again, I was shocked by
how frail she looked. A lot of the good memories about her
came flooding back: how excited she'd been to be a grandmother when John was born, the look of joy and contentment
on her face when she'd held Alan in her arms for the first time,
how she hadn't judged me when I told her about my affair with
Fernie.

We slowly began building a new, healthy mother-daughter
relationship, and in November she finally apologized to me
for her role in everything that had happened between us. I'd
waited all my life for this. She held me in her arms and cried,
saying, "I love you, my *chiquita*." It was the best Mom could
do. I understood this. She just didn't know how to love. She'd
missed out on so much because my grandmother hadn't allowed her to have a relationship with her own father. We both
had. That short time when Grandpa had been in our lives was
the first time I'd felt a true sense of belonging, that I was part

of a real family. Both of our lives could have been so different had he lived longer or been a presence in my mother's life throughout her childhood. It's heartbreaking, really.

Through this, Little Nikki has been growing up too, making the decision to release my perpetrators and leave my past behind. By finding self-love, I was able to reparent that shy, scared little girl, extending loving arms to her and promising that I would be the nurturing, protective mother that she needed. Every now and then, Little Nikki is filled with anger about injustices, but it is then that my warrior self, the fierce, protective mother part of me, comes alive. I can rise up and speak out about injustice; Little Nikki no longer has to suffer alone in silence.

**

Reconnecting with my mother prompted me to reach out to the Robles side of the family, whom I'd lost touch with. I wanted to know why they hadn't stayed in touch with my mother, so I called Aunt Alice. She was surprised but gracious and invited me to Thanksgiving. I was overjoyed to be with all of them again.

In December 2021, Mom and I shared our first Christmas in many years. We went to Rob's home, and then I invited all of them to be my guests for the day at a resort in Gaylord, Texas. We ate at the buffet, sang Christmas carols, and got massages. For the first time, Mom opened up to me a little bit about being abused as a child, though it wasn't easy for her to talk about. I just listened. I knew this was a big step for her, and I didn't want to do anything that would stop her from sharing her truth with me. The horrors she'd gone through were so similar to my own. I sympathized with her and understood that she was not emotionally able to offer that which she had never received. She is still struggling to forgive her own mother.

It's not perfect between us, but when Mom's angry and shouts or says hurtful things, I just try not to react. I know it is not about me. Importantly, she no longer holds power over me. Forgiveness set me free. And I found my way to forgiveness for myself, rather than for my mom or anyone else.

EPILOGUE

Throughout my life, I've made a lot of bad choices, ones that have caused me deep emotional trauma. I never felt good enough. I was always looking to external sources for validation and approval. This prompted me to turn over my power, whether it was to my mother or to the men I was in relationships with. I blamed myself for allowing others to mistreat me and accepted toxic and dysfunctional relationships, especially with my mom and romantic partners. I never felt at peace.

This created many problems in other areas of my personal life. When I was a child, Mom would not let me express the anger I felt toward her for mistreating me, so I repressed it. Anger is a force and can be directed in only two ways—inward or outward. I learned I had disconnected from all my anger toward my initial traumatizers and turned it on myself. And by doing this, it produced all kinds of unpleasant feelings: shame, guilt, self-blame, and so many others. I then later had difficulty expressing anger, even when it was appropriate. Internalized anger became self-loathing, poor self-care, and active self-harm. I had poor self-control, poor boundaries, and poor impulse control, which led me to affairs, compulsive shopping, and alcohol and opioid addiction. Back then I did not understand where my self-loathing was coming from. Somehow, subconsciously, I would end up finding reasons to hate myself.

I believed that I'd deserved all the mistreatment I'd received as a child.

It's taken me many years of counseling to understand that I'm not to blame for being sexually abused as a child. When I finally processed my feelings about this with Renee many years later, I was able to see none of it was my fault. I no longer blame myself for having failed to resist these sexual attacks. None of my innocent responses to feelings of pleasure and stimulation entailed consent. How could I consent? I was just a little girl.

I've also struggled to understand my abusers, the predators who stole my innocence, my childhood. I've often wondered if my step-uncle was a victim of sexual abuse when he was a child. I've done research and discovered that, in so many dysfunctional families, the abused grow up to become the abusers, and the fact that my step-grandpa fondled me too leads me to suspect that my step-uncle was once the target of his deviant affections. Not that this excuses what he did to me, but it does help make some sense of everything.

We were all links in this chain of wounded souls, all carrying this shame that pushed us to make unhealthy decisions for ourselves and the people around us. I imagine there was some machismo playing a role here too. If my step-uncle was, in fact, molested, he would never have been able to admit that or seek help without it feeling like a show of weakness. That culture of toxic masculinity—especially prevalent in the Latino community but also visible in so many other cultures—ensured these family cycles of abuse would continue in silence, unbroken across generations. I have lived this in my marriages. I believe we need more social awareness programs for machismo, which is conducive to violence, and violence is at an all-time high in the Latino community. Our laws should address this pervasive behavior. It should be studied. It could save someone's life. We women need to rise up and take a stand.

Research has shown that women who have been sexually abused have a twelve- to twentyfold increase in suicide attempts. With child sexual abuse, there is a 150 percent increased risk of later suicidal behavior. There is also a correlation between domestic violence victims and suicide attempts. Statistics show that suicides among girls and women increased by 50 percent between 2000 and 2016, and another study revealed that most women seeking protection orders have experienced suicidal thoughts or behaviors. More importantly, coercive control as a form of abuse has been implicated as the highest predictor of suicidal behavior in a survivor of intimate partner violence (IPV). A 2005 study by Dutton and Goodman reports that coercive control creates feelings of hopelessness in survivors, which leads to suicide as a fast way to end the abuse. It can also lead to multiple psychological disorders, including, but not limited to, PTSD, depression, bipolar disorder, and schizophrenia. I believe the links between suicide and IPV must be explored more closely.

I also want to bring awareness to unhealthy spending patterns, which can be destructive and can quickly spiral out of control. It comes from an inner need to fill a void, one that can only be filled when we begin to love ourselves and connect with others on a deeper level. This is why we need to create social awareness programs about the importance of operating interdependently, rather than codependently. We also need to stand up against coercive control—through campaigning and reaching out to officials at the local, state, and federal level. Of course, women can be controlling too, but when the offender is a man, coercive control exploits and reinforces sexual inequalities in the larger society in ways that make it far more devastating than when women are controlling. Legislation should place a priority on the safety and well-being of women, complemented by an emphasis on liberty, autonomy, dignity, and equality. To fully grasp how various forms of subjugation harm women, we must first recognize that women have the same rights to personhood as men. I do feel women need to advocate and continue to lean in when it comes to domestic violence, but for some, the trauma of their experiences makes it difficult to speak out. Violence is not a public topic that victims eagerly discuss, as it opens them up not only to retraumatization but also to ridicule and disbelief from others.

Coercive control laws could help domestic violence abuse victims too. They need to be able to protect themselves, because sometimes their perpetrators are never held accountable. Women who kill their abusers can be labeled as having battered woman syndrome, as was the case with my aunt who killed two of her intimate partners. And yet in other cases, women have no legal recourse, enduring horrendous mental abuse from husbands or intimate partners who use controlling and coercive behaviors to take complete power over them—just as Gerardo had done in my life, making me totally dependent on him. While some foreign countries provide coercive control protection, in the United States only a handful of states do. So we must continue to advocate at local, state, and federal levels to enact coercive control laws to protect the most vulnerable.

I also want to speak on the links between racialized and gender-based violence. Many marginalized communities remain underserved and neglected when it comes to police and the law. While studies vary, most tend to agree that women of color face the highest levels of abuse and therefore are more often the recipients of its deadly consequences. Women such as immigrants and refugees, those who have less income or less access to their income, and those who are trans or gender nonconforming are very much a target of hate, violence, and biased treatment. They must constantly battle with policies that do not include them. The very ones in the line of duty also often fail us; I feel that police need to be trained to recognize the patterns of women who may be in danger of being abused. This issue is even more important for women of color, many of whom are afraid to call the police because they know the color of their skin makes them a target of police violence. Mental health and domestic violence advocates should be more accessible in these cases so perpetrators can be held accountable and women can have support as they rebuild their lives.

Our society would benefit from a more open and honest approach to these issues. We need to empower victims of domestic violence by creating awareness and a safe space to speak out about our personal experiences with IPV and other forms of violence that are experienced so prevalently but rarely discussed.

Other poor choices I have made relate to my medical treatment. I surrendered my patient rights without truly understanding the harms of opioid medications that I then became addicted to. Request information and fully participate in your own health treatment! Informed consent for medical care ensures that your medical provider has given you all the information about your condition along with testing and treatment options before you carefully consider a decision related to your health and body. If you are to receive medication, ensure you have full knowledge of your diagnosis and the pros and cons of your treatments. You have control and final say about what goes in your body, no matter what the doctor says.

Finally, I had to learn the difference between caregiving and caretaking: both are expressions of kindness and love, but there are some key differences between them. As a caretaker, I would begin trying to fix my mother's problems as soon as they arose. Now, as a caregiver, I empathize fully, letting her know she is not alone, and I lovingly ask, "What can you do about the problem, Mom?" instead of asking her what I can do. I have shifted the *I* to the *you*, and that lessens the enabling behavior of being a caretaker.

As a caregiver, I also practice self-care unabashedly because I know that keeping myself happy enables me to be of service to others. Caretaking created anxiety and depression for me in the past. I was giving too much. Caregiving, on the other hand, decreases anxiety and depression and fills me up. And this is something I had to learn and set boundaries around. Caregiving is an expression of kindness and love. Caretaking is a dysfunctional learned behavior that can be changed. As a caretaker, I attracted needy people. Now, in caregiving, I attract healthy people, and we can support each other.

Perhaps the simplest explanation is that as my mother's former caretaker, I tended to be judgmental, and in caregiving, I do not see the logic in judging others, including my mom. Today, I am no longer a caretaker, because that took a lot away from me. I practice a "live and let live" attitude. Caretaking leaves us feeling stressed, exhausted, and frustrated. Caregiving feels right and resembles love. Taking care of my mom at Christmas this past year truly reenergized and inspired me.

Life is about choices. We can remain trapped in the cycle of making bad choices, or we can release the past, forgive, move on, and birth a new transformation, a new creation. I am no longer a captive of my own thoughts, which have been so negative since early childhood and all through my life. It is freeing to release myself from that negativity and love myself.

I want to be remembered as someone who stood up for women's rights to self-autonomy and freedom from oppression. It is a privilege to speak openly about the abuse I have suffered, because if it helps even just one person going through something similar, my pain has served a purpose. If you are experiencing any kind of abuse, know you are not nearly as alone as you may feel. You are worthy of a life of happiness. You can become free.

I'm still working on standing on my own. But it is so empowering to give myself full credit for being the woman that I am today. I have been many women in my lifetime. I have been the nurturer, the provider. I have been the lover and the fighter. But the woman that I value the most will always be the survivor.

ACKNOWLEDGMENTS

I would like to thank Jesus, my savior, as well as my sons, for loving me for who I am and who I was before coming to my Christian faith. For me, God, Jesus, spirituality, and faith mean offering acts of selfless, unconditional love for the battered, the broken, the crushed in spirit, the abused, the poor, and the hurting hearts, binding wounds with love. I provide a ministry of service in which I extend myself to those in need. This goes far beyond a brick-and-mortar church. It does not stop on Sundays. Rather, always giving back to my community through selfless acts of giving—no matter the area—allows me to help a battered or abused soul. Love knows no distance or barrier. Love encompasses souls; love transcends the unimaginable. Love heals.

To my therapist, Renee, I am forever grateful to you.

To some very special sisters in Christ: Joanie, Sandy, Rachel, and Regi. Thank you for walking with me side by side and sharing true moments of sisterhood. Some from afar, yet close enough to show your love, support, and encouragement.

To me, family came much later in life. Some family is not of blood but of a heart that knows the love of Christ. It does not matter if you are related to someone by DNA; the heart can truly and deeply love a brother or sister of faith, and that love pours out to reach the brokenhearted, the oppressed, and the crushed in spirit, as it did for me.

Finally, my heart, my love, goes out to all women who have experienced any kind of trauma or wounding in their lives. I have fought this battle of abuse since I was a child, and I encourage my fellow abuse survivors to keep fighting until you achieve victory and safety.

Much love,

Nikki

RESOURCES

If you are experiencing intimate partner violence or another form of domestic abuse, help is available 24-7 through the National Domestic Violence Hotline: 800-799-7233.

For more information about how to get help, please go to my website, https://traumabooknikki.com/.

Below is a list of sources I used in researching this book:

https://abcnews.go.com/Health/female-suicide-rate-jumps
-50-percent-2000/story?id=55906336
https://www.afs4kids.org/blog/29-surprising-foster-care
-facts/
https://alcoholtreatment.niaaa.nih.gov/what-to-know
/alcohol-use-disorder
https://www.amazon.com/dp/0877846081/
https://www.apa.org/monitor/2014/11/suicide-violence
https://www.apa.org/monitor/2019/01/numbers
https://bmcpublichealth.biomedcentral.com/articles/10.1186
/s12889-021-12232-3
https://books.google.com/books?id=VzYpatFxuoQC
https://www.center4research.org/childhood-youth
-experiences-link-suicide/
https://www.childwelfare.gov/pubpdfs/child-trauma.pdf
https://www.compellingtruth.org/spiritual-strongholds.html

https://discovery.ucl.ac.uk/id/eprint/10135084/10/Osrin
_JIV_21_230_accepted_version.pdf

https://www.expressivecounseling.com/articles
/codependency-caretaking

https://fosteringperspectives.org/fp_v10n1/trauma.htm

https://www.hrc.org/resources/fatal-violence-against-the
-transgender-and-gender-non-conforming-community
-in-2021

https://www.iasa-dmm.org/images/uploads/Penelope
%20Trickett%20sexual%20abuse(1).pdf

https://iwpr.org/iwpr-issues/race-ethnicity-gender-and
-economy/violence-against-black-women-many-types
-far-reaching-effects/

https://link.springer.com/article/10.1007/s11199-005-4196-6

https://www2.ljworld.com/news/2011/dec/05/mind-matters
-parental-mirroring-provides-child-sen/

https://magazine.medlineplus.gov/article/confronting
-alcohol-use-disorder-and-misconceptions-as-a-woman

https://maxlucado.com/strongholds/

https://medlineplus.gov/opioidmisuseandaddiction.html

https://moneyfit.org/impulse-spending

https://www.ncbi.nlm.nih.gov/pmc/articles/PMC1805733/

https://www.ncbi.nlm.nih.gov/pmc/articles/PMC5658049/

https://www.new-hope.org/facts-about-domestic-violence/

https://www.niaaa.nih.gov/publications/brochures-and-fact
-sheets/understanding-alcohol-use-disorder

https://www.npr.org/sections/health-shots/2018/06
/14/619338703/u-s-suicides-rates-are-rising-faster
-among-women-than-men

https://www.nytimes.com/2017/12/02/opinion/sunday/the
-cost-of-devaluing-women.html

https://psychcentral.com/blog/what-makes-a-family
-functional-vs-dysfunctional

https://www.psychologytoday.com/us/blog/resolution-not
-conflict/201303/how-contempt-destroys-relationships

https://www.psychologytoday.com/us/blog/science-choice
/201806/5-patterns-compulsive-buying

https://www.psychologytoday.com/us/blog/toxic
-relationships/201809/why-men-are-aggressive
-against-women-and-the-damage-it-causes

https://psycnet.apa.org/record/2005-10227-003

https://pubmed.ncbi.nlm.nih.gov/27456533/

https://www.rit.edu/liberalarts/sites/rit.edu.liberalarts/files
/documents/our-work/2009-12.pdf

https://www.saferresource.org.au/the_bible_on_domestic
_family_violence

https://sites.uab.edu/humanrights/2019/02/22/invisible-no
-more-police-violence-against-black-women-and
-women-of-color/

https://www.tandfonline.com/doi/full/10.1080/10926771
.2016.1214937

https://www.thegospelcoalition.org/themelios/review
/women-in-ministry-four-views/

https://www.thehelpsavefoundation.org/about-us/domestic
-violence-statistics/

https://theshulmancenter.com/overspending-shopping
-addiction.html

https://www.usatoday.com/story/news/health/2020/09/11
/youth-suicide-rate-increases-cdc-report-finds
/3463549001/

https://www.verywellmind.com/domestic-violence-varies-by
-ethnicity-62648

https://www.verywellmind.com/what-is-compulsive
-shopping-disorder-2510592

https://victimsofcrime.org/child-sexual-abuse-statistics/

https://www.webmd.com/depression/news/20200911
/suicide-rate-keeps-rising-among-young-americans
https://www.webmd.com/mental-health/dissociative
-identity-disorder-multiple-personality-disorder
https://www.who.int/news/item/09-09-2019-suicide-one
-person-dies-every-40-seconds

ABOUT THE AUTHOR

Nikki Navarro overcame adversity, trauma, and minimal education to become a successful real estate agent in 2002. In 2017, she began her own real estate business flipping and rehabbing houses, where she specializes in providing families with beautiful homes and a loving safe haven. She is passionate about empowering women and shares her story with the hope of helping others fight against the injustices they face.